Letts

KT-475-515

revise
GCSE

David Floyd

Business
Studies

Contents

The business environment

Business organisations

The structure of organisations

Supporting and controlling business activity

Managing human resources

Finance and accounting

Marketing

Production

This book and your GCSE course

	AQA A	AQA B	AQA B short course	EDEXCEL	EDEXCEL short course
Syllabus number	3132	3133	3139	1503	
Terminal papers	One written paper 75%	Two written papers, 37.5% each	One written paper 75%	One written paper 75%	One written paper 75%
Coursework	25%	(or alternative written paper) 25%	(or alternative written paper) 25%	25%	25%
			SPECIFICATION REFERENCE NUMBERS		
The business environment					
Economic systems	1	1	1	1.1, 1.2	1.1
Population, employment location of industry	1	1	1	1.3	1.2
The EU and international issues	1	1	1	1.3	1.3
Controlling and supporting business activity	1, 4	1	1	1.4, 1.5	1.3, 1.4
Business organisations					
Private and public sectors, stakeholders	2	2, 3	2, 3	1.6, 1.7, 1.8	1.5, 1.6
Internal organisation and communication	2, 4	2, 4	2	2.1, 2.2	1.5
Change, size and growth	1, 2, 4	2		1.2, 1.7	1.6
Business functional areas					
Human relations	4	4		2.3–2.6	2
Finance	3	5	4	3.1–3.5	3
Marketing	3	7	6	4.1, 4.2	4
Production	2, 3	6	5	5.1–5.3	5

Visit your awarding body for full details of your course or download your complete GCSE specifications.

STAY YOUR COURSE!

Use these pages to get to know your course

- Make sure you know your exam board
- Check which specification you are doing

- Know how your course is assessed:
  - What format are the papers?
  - How is coursework assessed?
  - How many papers are there?

OCR A	OCR B	OCR A short course	WJEC	NICCEA
1951	1952	1051		
One core paper 50% plus one option paper 25%	Three written papers, 25% each	One written paper 75%	One written paper 75%	Two written papers, 30% and 50%
(or alternative written paper) 25%	25%	(or alternative written paper) 25%	25%	20%
SPECIFICATION REFERENCE NUMBERS				
Core 1	1 and 2, 3	1	1	1
Core 1, option 1	3	1	1	1
Core 1, option 1	3	1	2	1
Core 5, option 1	3	1	2	1
Core 2	1 and 2, 3, 4	1, 2, 3	1, 2	1
Core 2, option 2	1 and 2	3	3	1
Core 2, option 1	1 and 2	5	3	1
Core 4	1 and 2, 3, 4	4	4	2
Core 2, core 3, option 1	1 and 2, 4	2, 3	7	5
Core 3, option 2	1 and 2, 4	3	6	4
Core 3, option 1	1 and 2, 4	3	5	3

Preparing for the examination

Planning your study

The final three months before taking your GCSE examination are very important in achieving your best grade. However, a good grade also depends on you **following an organised approach** throughout your course.

- After completing a topic in school or college, go through the topic again in the *Letts Revise GCSE Business Studies Study Guide*. Copy out the main points again on a sheet of paper, or use a **highlighter pen** to emphasise them.
- A couple of days later, try to **write out these key points** from memory. Check **differences** between what you wrote originally and what you wrote later.
- If you have written your notes on a piece of paper, keep this for revision later.
- **Try some questions** in the book and **check your answers**.
- Decide whether you have fully **mastered the topic** and write down any weaknesses you think you have.

Preparing a revision programme

In the last three months before the final examination, go through the list of topics in your Examination Board's specification to **identify those topics you feel the need to concentrate on**. It is tempting to spend valuable revision time on the areas you already know well, but balance this with time spent improving your knowledge of other business studies topics.

When you feel you have mastered all the topics, **spend time trying past questions**. Each time check your answers with the answers given. In the final couple of weeks **go back to your summary sheets** (or highlighting in the book).

How this book will help you

Letts Revise GCSE Business Studies Study Guide will help you because:

- it contains the **essential content** for your GCSE course without the extra material that will not be examined
- it contains **Progress Checks** and GCSE questions to help you confirm your understanding
- it gives **sample GCSE questions** with summary answers and advice from an examiner on how to improve the answer
- examination questions from 2003 are different from those in 2002 or 2001, and the questions in this book have been written by experienced examiners who are writing the questions for 2003 and beyond
- **comments in the margin** and **highlighted key points** will draw your attention to important points you might miss otherwise

Five ways to improve your grade

1 Read the question carefully

Many students fail to answer the actual question set. Perhaps they misread the question, or answer a similar one they have studied during revision. To avoid doing this, **read the question once right through**, then **re-read it more slowly**. Some students underline or **highlight** key words as they read through the question. Questions set for GCSE Business Studies often contain a lot of information, which you should use in your answer by **applying** your general business studies knowledge to this specific information.

2 Give enough detail

If a part of a question is worth, say, three marks, you should normally make three points: these may be different content points, or you may have to expand and develop a single point. Be careful that you do not make the same point three times, because there are **no marks for repetition**.

3 Quality of written communication

From 2003, some marks on GCSE papers are given for the quality of your written communication. This includes correct sentence structure and correct use of business studies terms.

4 Use of business studies language

There is an important business studies vocabulary you should use. Try to use the **correct business terms** in your answers and **spell** them correctly (including the word 'business' itself!). As you revise, it is worth making a list of business terms you meet and checking that you understand the meaning of these terms.

5 Show your working

It is likely that you will have to do calculations in some questions, for example those on the accounts section of the specification. You should always **show your workings** in full. Then, if you make an arithmetical mistake, you may still receive marks for correct business studies knowledge.

Coursework

Coursework is not normally limited to tasks you can complete at your desk. It encourages you to be aware of business activities through local study, display some evidence of originality, and collect, select and use your business knowledge in appropriate ways.

Your coursework topic may be set by your Examining Group. For example, EDEXCEL sets several coursework topics, from which its candidates select one to complete. Even if this is the case, you will have to **relate the general topic**, e.g. franchising, business communication, financial performance or marketing media, **to a specific situation**.

When planning your coursework, consider these points.

1 Select an appropriate organisation or situation

Teachers sometimes find that their students choose coursework topics that are over-ambitious or too wide-ranging, or they may be based on an organisation about which it is difficult to obtain facts and figures.

2 Choose a topic that demonstrates the right skills

You need to:
- **obtain** information
- **analyse** this information
- **summarise** your findings
- **present** your findings

The 'personal' skills you will need include an ability to research, to solve problems, to integrate different business studies ideas and content, and to persevere with a long-lasting piece of work.

3 The topic must lead you to produce your own work

This means that you won't get many marks for simply copying out lots of information from brochures, leaflets or websites. This is the work of others: if you include 'secondary' material, remember to interpret and apply it to the situation that you're researching.

Remember that, although your teacher can't do your coursework for you, he or she will be able to offer you **advice**.

The business environment

The following topics are included in this chapter:

- ● **Activity in our economy**
- ● **Economic systems**
- ● **Population and employment**
- ● **The location of industry**
- ● **International trade**

1.1 Activity in our economy

LEARNING SUMMARY

After studying this section you should be able to understand:

- ● **the factors of production**
- ● **how and why specialisation takes place**

Economic activity

AQA A   AQA B
EDEXCEL
OCR A   OCR B
WJEC
NICCEA

Economic activity takes place within a country such as the United Kingdom. It sets out to **satisfy the needs of the society**. The economy produces the goods and services demanded by its members – its **consumers** – and it takes **resources** to do this. We know these resources by the name **factors of production**.

Fig. 1.1 The four factors of production

The four factors of production are:

1. **capital**, used to invest in the machines, equipment and companies that all contribute to producing resources

2. **enterprise**, which refers to the people who are willing to take the risk of setting up in business and of making business decisions

3. **land**, which is used for agriculture, houses, leisure activities and so on, as well as for providing natural resources like iron ore and other minerals

4. **labour**, the number of men and women who are available to work

> 'Land' in economics also includes the sea and its natural resources (e.g. fish and oil).

Scarcity and choice

One of the main problems faced by any society is that it can't satisfy all the wants of its members. These **wants are unlimited**, and there are **limited resources** to meet them. We don't have an endless supply of the factors of production, which means we have to make a series of choices about:

- **what** will be produced
- **how** it will be produced
- **where** it will be produced

In many cases the **price mechanism** (page 12) determines **what** is produced, or the **government** may take an important role here. When planning **how** to produce goods and services, entrepreneurs try to combine the other factors of production as efficiently as possible: in modern economies, for example, employees (**labour**) have often been replaced with machines (**capital**) to make production more efficient and less expensive. The availability and position of the factors of production – such as where we can find skilled labour and inexpensive land – will be a major influence in deciding **where** firms produce their goods and services.

> **KEY POINT**
>
> Governments often use regional policy to influence where new firms are established, for example by awarding grants to encourage entrepreneurs to set up production in certain regions of the country.

Opportunity cost

Because we have limited resources and unlimited wants, some of our wants have to be **unsatisfied**. We must choose how we spend our money or our time. If you have the choice of, say, going to the cinema or going bowling, by deciding to go to the cinema you've had to give up the chance to go bowling. The **opportunity cost** of the cinema is going bowling: it is the cost of having to go without one thing to get another.

This is exactly the same choice that entrepreneurs, and society in general, must make because resources are limited. For an entrepreneur, the opportunity cost of, say, buying a new machine may be having to postpone the manufacture of a new model in the product range.

Specialisation

AQA A   AQA B
EDEXCEL
OCR A   OCR B
WJEC
NICCEA

> Specialising in what we do well leads to greater efficiency and higher economic output.

In advanced economies such as ours, production tends to be **indirect** rather than direct. This means that people do not produce things for themselves, but instead work with others to make goods and services that are then sold to the general public.

Firms also specialise: a **division of labour** takes place, with employees specialising in different jobs. This allows the firm to use complicated machinery and production processes, with work becoming divided into different **functions**, represented by the main departments (production, sales, buying, etc.) that are staffed by specialists.

Interdependence: specialisation of firms

The various 'parts' that make up an economy start to depend on each other as a result of specialisation. Firms become dependent on other firms for their **input**, or to assist them in selling their **output**. For example, a farmer specialising in growing vegetables will rely on others to distribute, pack and sell these vegetables to the final consumer; and a car manufacturer relies on the expertise of an advertising agency to promote the cars and on garages to sell them.

> We find exceptions to this rule: for instance, many car manufacturers sell directly to the public through the Internet.

Specialisation of countries

Countries also specialise. In many cases, what they specialise in depends on their **climate** and **natural resources**: examples include Bolivia and tin production; many Mediterranean countries and tourism; South Africa and gold mining. There may be **historical influences**, such as the development of banking and financial services in Great Britain.

> Our history has been one important factor in helping the UK establish such a strong service sector.

A country is therefore not self-sufficient. It has to trade with other countries to get the range of goods and services its population needs, and which it cannot provide for itself. **International trade** (page 25) takes place, which increases the interdependence between countries.

Specialisation of people

People become trained for different occupations, such as teacher, nurse, welder and insurance clerk. Regardless of the type of work they do, these people will have similar wants: clothes, washing machines, houses, and specialist services such as plumbing or TV repairs. People therefore have to **depend on others** to provide them with these goods and services. This **interdependence** relies on the use of **money** to buy the various goods and services demanded.

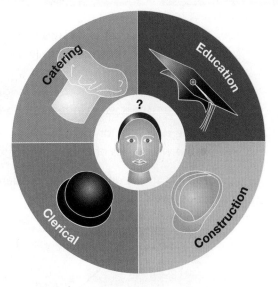

Fig. 1.2 Specialisation of people

The **advantages** of specialisation are that:

1. **unit costs are reduced**, because manufacturing processes can take place more easily
2. **specialist equipment** can be used, leading to more efficient production
3. **employees become specialised**, and therefore quicker and more efficient

The **disadvantages** of specialisation are that:

1. there is the risk of **boredom** for some employees, leading to **lower job satisfaction** and possibly labour disputes or lower-quality production
2. a single group of workers taking industrial action can **halt the production line**
3. unemployed workers may possess narrow, specialist but **out-of-date skills**

PROGRESS CHECK

1. The **four** factors of production are _____ , _____ , _____ and _____ .
2. What **three** decisions must be made in an economy?
3. In what ways do economies specialise?

3. By firms; by countries; by people.
2. What to produce; how to produce; where to produce.
1. Land; labour; capital; enterprise.

1.2 Economic systems

LEARNING SUMMARY

After studying this section you should be able to understand:

- *the market economy*
- *the planned economy*
- *the mixed economy*
- *the three production sectors of the UK economy*

The 'free market' system

AQA A   AQA B
EDEXCEL
OCR A   OCR B
WJEC
NICCEA

This is also known as the **market** system, the **capitalist** system, or the **laissez-faire** system. In a truly 'free' system there is no interference from the government in the workings of the economy. In a free market economy, **resources are owned by individuals** and not by the State. The **price mechanism** is its main feature. The **prices** of goods and services are set by:

- the **demand** for them from the consumers
- the willingness of the producers to **supply** these goods and services

Fig. 1.3 shows different levels of demand and supply existing at different price levels.

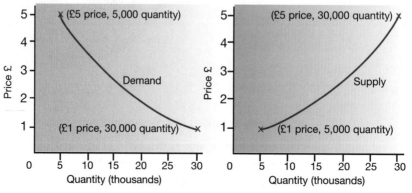

Fig. 1.3 Demand and supply curves

The curves show us that a price of £5 will lead to 30 000 being supplied, but only 5000 being demanded. However, if the price of the item was only £1, the demand level would be 30 000 with only 5000 being supplied.

Demand and supply **interact**. If demand exceeds supply (as in Fig. 1.3, when the price is £1), the price will tend to rise. Higher prices reduce the overall demand for the item, because some people will not pay – or can't afford – the higher price. Higher prices also encourage greater supply: the higher price means a higher profit margin, encouraging firms to make and sell more, and new firms enter the market. As a result, supply will eventually meet demand.

If the supply level of a product is greater than the demand for it, its price will fall. More people can now afford it, which will increase its demand: fewer products are likely to be made because of the lower price, and so the supply level will fall to meet the new level of demand.

The various factors of production also depend on the workings of the price mechanism. If the price of labour is too high, it may not be employed (demanded) by firms. If the rate of interest for bank loans – a form of capital – falls, more loans will be demanded by firms.

Features of the free market system

- **Incentive**. People are encouraged to work hard because there is the opportunity to create personal wealth.
- **Choice**. People can spend their money how they wish: they can set up their own business, or choose for whom they want to work.
- **Competition**. Through competition, less efficient producers are priced out of the market, and more efficient producers supply products at lower prices for the consumers by using the factors of production more efficiently. The factors of production which are no longer needed can be used elsewhere. Competition also stimulates new ideas.

BUT

- **Unequal distribution of wealth**. The wealthier members of society tend to hold most of the economic and political power, whilst the poorer members of society have much less influence. Sometimes production concentrates on the luxury items demanded by the rich.
- **Public services**. The price mechanism doesn't always work efficiently when services such as defence, education and health need to be provided for the benefit of society as a whole.
- **Profit motive**. Since the profit motive is all-important to producers, they may ignore social costs of production, such as pollution. Short-term profit performance may be considered more important than long-term growth.
- **Hardship**. In theory, factors of production like labour are 'mobile' and can be switched from one use to another: in practice, this is difficult and may lead to hardship through unemployment. It also means that these factors are being wasted by not being used.
- **Wasted competition**. Some firms may use expensive advertising to sell 'new' products that are almost identical to many other products currently on sale. Other firms may control the market, choosing to restrict supply so prices remain high, or may agree with other suppliers the price to charge: as a result, price will not be determined by the interaction of supply and demand.

Skills that are in very scarce supply but in high demand in our economy (such as those of top–class athletes or artists) command extremely high pay rates.

Many recent 'hi–tech' developments, such as the way mobile phones are changing, are due to tremendous competition in the marketplace.

Companies nowadays value a good public image: they often try to develop this by publicising the positive work they do for the environment.

The government encourages competition through bodies such as the Competition Commission, and through laws.

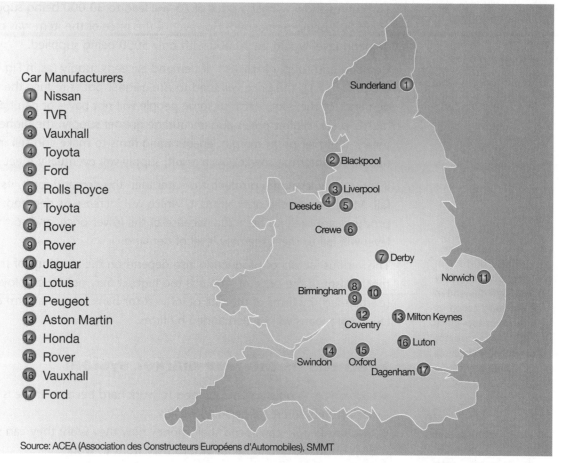

Car Manufacturers

1. Nissan
2. TVR
3. Vauxhall
4. Toyota
5. Ford
6. Rolls Royce
7. Toyota
8. Rover
9. Rover
10. Jaguar
11. Lotus
12. Peugeot
13. Aston Martin
14. Honda
15. Rover
16. Vauxhall
17. Ford

Source: ACEA (Association des Constructeurs Européens d'Automobiles), SMMT

Fig. 1.4 Free enterprise: choice provided by car manufacturers in England

KEY POINT

In practice, there are no economies in the world that are entirely 'market'.

The planned economy

AQA A   AQA B
EDEXCEL
OCR A   OCR B
WJEC
NICCEA

Also known as the **command** or the **collectivist** system, the planned system **relies exclusively on the State**. The government decides what is made, how it is made, how much of it is made and how distribution takes place. Resources – the factors of production – are controlled by the government on behalf of both producers and consumers, and price levels are fixed by the government rather than through the operation of supply and demand.

Planned economies tend to be more self-sufficient, and take part in less international trade, than market economies.

Features of the planned system

- **Use of resources**. Central planning can lead to the full use of all the factors of production, so reducing or ending unemployment.
- **Large-scale production**. Economies of scale become possible due to mass production taking place.
- **Public services**. 'Natural monopolies' such as the supply of power, or defence, can be provided efficiently through central planning.

- **Basic services**. There is less emphasis on providing luxuries for the rich, and greater concentration on producing a range of goods and services for all the population. There may be less of a difference in wealth and income between the richer and poorer members of society.

BUT

- **Lack of choice**. Consumers have less influence over what is made, and they may have less say in what they do as a career.
- **Little incentive**. Since competition between producers isn't as fierce as in a market economy, there is little incentive to improve how things are made or how people work. Employees are not given real incentives to work harder, and so production levels may be lower than in a free enterprise economy.
- **Centralised control**. Because the State makes the major decisions, government departments are large and influential: the existence of such a powerful **bureaucracy** can lead to inefficient planning and to problems of communication, and government officials may use their power for personal gain rather than for the good of the rest of society.

> **KEY POINT**
>
> **The well-known 'communist' economies, such as China and those we used to find in Russia and Eastern Europe, are becoming (or have become) much more market-based.**

The mixed economy

In practice, all economies are 'mixed', containing some elements of both of the other forms of economy. Most modern 'western economies', like ours or that of the USA, are mainly market-based economies, but we still find a heavy government involvement through planning areas such as defence and education. In recent years, our economy has become more market-based through the government **privatising** (page 43) old State monopolies.

The mixed economy includes elements of both market and planned economies. The government operates the **public sector**, including local authorities and national services such as health. The **private sector** is left largely to the price mechanism and 'market forces', although in practice it is **regulated** by various laws (see Chapter 4).

The advantages of the mixed economy are:

- **Necessary services are provided**. In a true market economy, services that failed to make a profit wouldn't be supplied.
- **Incentive**. Since there is a private sector where individuals can make a lot of money, incentives still exist in a mixed economy.
- **Competition**. Prices are kept low through competition taking place.

Just as the mixed system gains from the 'best of both worlds', it can also suffer from the disadvantages of both the market and planned systems. For example, **large monopolies** are still found in the private sector, so competition doesn't really take place. Also, since there will be a public sector in a mixed economy, we may also find a lot of **bureaucracy** ('red tape').

Primary, secondary and tertiary production

AQA A   AQA B
EDEXCEL
OCR A   OCR B
WJEC
NICCEA

People in less advanced economies often satisfy their wants **directly** by providing the goods and services they need themselves. We know that, as countries develop economically, increased specialisation and the division of labour lead to **indirect** production, workers being paid in money for their part in the production process. The money they earn can be used to buy the goods and services they want.

The firms that we find in these more advanced economies will be involved in **production**, which is classified under the three headings in Fig.1.5.

Primary production

All primary production involves some sort of **extraction**. Areas of work in the primary sector of our economy are:

1. mining and quarrying
2. fishing
3. farming
4. forestry

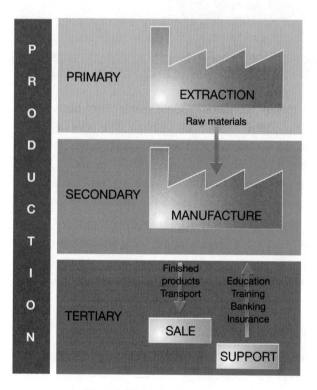

Fig. 1.5 Types of production

Secondary production

Firms taking part in secondary production are involved in either **manufacturing** or in **construction**.

- These firms manufacture a finished article such as a car, or make parts that are used in assembling the finished product (e.g. suppliers of parts that go in the car's engine).
- A firm in the secondary sector may also be involved in construction: building houses, roads, or 'one-off' projects such as a bridge.

Tertiary production

We also find direct services provided for the community: these include occupations such as teachers, fire fighters, the police and the health service.

Items that have been grown, extracted, made or built still have to get to the final consumer. Although the producer may sell the items directly to consumers – e.g. a farmer selling farm produce in a farm shop, or a manufacturer selling directly over the Internet – we still find that most products need to be transported, stored, advertised, financed in some way and insured. There is a wide range of commercial services and activities making up tertiary production – the **service sector** of the UK – which we can see in Fig. 1.6.

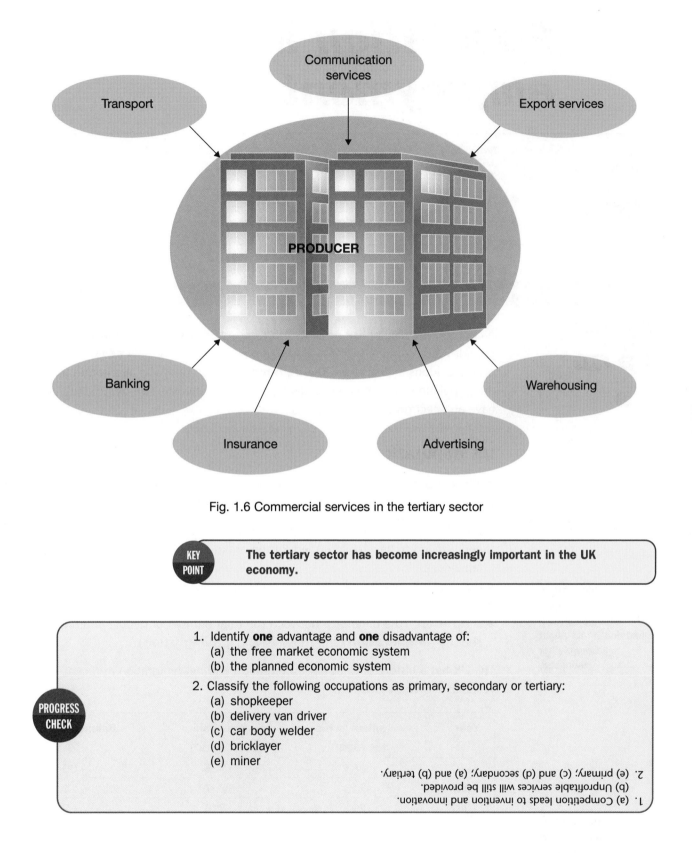

Fig. 1.6 Commercial services in the tertiary sector

> **KEY POINT**
>
> The tertiary sector has become increasingly important in the UK economy.

PROGRESS CHECK

1. Identify **one** advantage and **one** disadvantage of:
   (a) the free market economic system
   (b) the planned economic system

2. Classify the following occupations as primary, secondary or tertiary:
   (a) shopkeeper
   (b) delivery van driver
   (c) car body welder
   (d) bricklayer
   (e) miner

1. (a) Competition leads to invention and innovation.
   (b) Unprofitable services will still be provided.
2. (e) primary; (c) and (d) secondary; (a) and (b) tertiary.

1.3 Population and employment

LEARNING SUMMARY

After studying this section you should be able to understand:

- *the UK population structure*
- *the nature of employment in the UK economy*
- *the different forms of unemployment found*

Population

AQA A AQA B EDEXCEL OCR A OCR B WJEC NICCEA

A country's population is one of its most important assets. The population provides the economy with the **entrepreneurs** and the supply **of labour** to produce goods and services. The **demand** for these products also comes from the population. Any change, therefore, in our population's size or structure will have an effect on our economy.

UK population

We hold a population **census** every ten years, to check changes in our population structure. The overall size of our population is influenced by:

- the **birth rate** – this depends on factors such as the number of women able and wishing to have children, education about parenthood, and attitudes to family size
- the **death rate** – influenced by factors such as living standards and medical advances
- **migration** – the difference between the total number of people entering a country (**immigration**) and those leaving it (**emigration**)

Our birth rate is about 13 children per thousand population, and death rate about 11 people per thousand.

The UK has a history of both net immigration and net emigration in recent years, as shown by Fig. 1.7.

Year	Inflow to the UK (000)	Outflow from the UK (000)	Balance
1997	285	225	+60
1992	216	227	−11
1987	212	210	+2

Fig. 1.7 Migration into and out of the UK (Source: ONS)

In recent years there has been a net 'brain drain' emigration of about 4000 professional and managerial people each year.

It isn't simply the number of people entering and leaving the UK that is important: we also need to consider the **skills** being brought into and leaving the country.

Population structure

Although the UK has a reasonably fixed total population, the **age structure** within this total is changing. Both government and business can use this information to **predict changes in demand for goods and services**. For example, the number of 15–19 year olds has fallen in recent years: this affects the number of people entering the labour market, and will therefore influence firms' recruitment policies. We believe there will be an increase in the number of over 60s to about 30% of the total population by 2038, compared with about 20% at present. This is likely to increase demand for products such as warmer clothing, smaller houses and flats, and public transport.

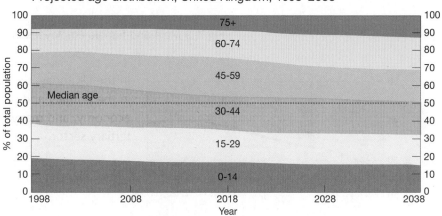

Projected age distribution, United Kingdom, 1998–2038

Fig. 1.8 UK population age trends (Source: ONS)

> **KEY POINT**
>
> **Problems of an ageing population include an increased demand for social services such as health services, and an increased dependence on those in work who must provide the tax and other contributions necessary to pay for these social services.**

Other national population trends include:

1. **more women than men** living in the UK at present (about 2 million)
2. a **drift of labour towards the south-east** of the country, encouraged by the opportunity of work but facing the problem of expensive housing and living costs

Employment and unemployment

Employment

In 1999 there were some 28.7 million employees in the UK, of whom just over half (16 million) were men. There were also over 3 million self-employed, of whom a quarter were women. The present features of our employment are a:

- growth in the number of women working
- growth in part-time and temporary jobs
- growth in the number of self-employed people
- fall in the number of men in full-time jobs

Fig. 1.9 illustrates the key trends.

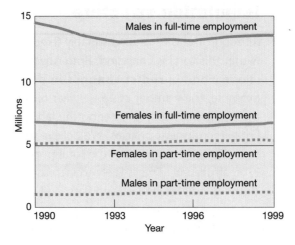

Fig. 1.9 Male and female employees in the UK (Source: ONS)

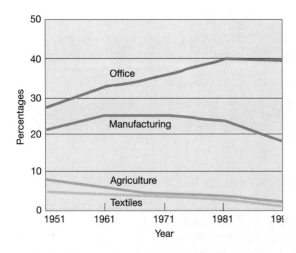

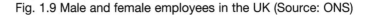

Fig. 1.10 Employee occupations in the UK (Source: ONS)

In the UK today, we also find fewer people employed in the primary and secondary sectors of the economy, and many more being employed in the tertiary sector.

Unemployment

This has often been a major economic problem in the UK in recent years. There are various types of unemployment affecting the different groups in the population, the various industries making up our economy, and the different regions of the country.

- **Frictional** unemployment is temporary and voluntary, occurring when **people change jobs**. It represents the time spent looking for a new job.
- **Structural** unemployment happens when there is a **long-term change in demand or supply**: for example, when a product or skill becomes out-of-date or unfashionable. Overseas competition has often led to UK companies becoming uncompetitive, with a resulting fall-off in the demand for this labour. As a result, structural unemployment has affected whole industries in the UK.
- **Cyclical** unemployment, often called 'demand deficient' unemployment, arises from a general **lack of demand** in the economy.
- **Seasonal** unemployment is found in industries such as tourism and agriculture, where the **seasonal nature of the work** leads to people becoming unemployed at certain times of the year.
- **Technological** unemployment arises from the fact that, in many industries, it is becoming possible to **substitute machines for people**: examples include the use of robots on production and assembly lines.

Steel, textiles, shipbuilding and cars are all industries that have suffered structural unemployment.

Groups at risk of being unemployed

Although we all face the risk of unemployment, certain groups or individuals stand a greater chance of becoming unemployed.

- **Age**. Younger workers entering the labour market may face problems in getting jobs and keeping them (e.g. they are less expensive to make redundant). Older people seeking employment are sometimes less willing to retrain to gain the new skills they may require.
- **Skill level**. Many jobs in the newer industries are for skilled or semi-skilled workers: many people made redundant from the older industries may have been doing unskilled work, or their skills are not longer required by these newer industries.
- **Discrimination**. In addition to possible discrimination by age, some employers discriminate on the grounds of race or ethnicity, sex, and disability.

> New industries have grown rapidly in recent years, the information technology and telecommunications industries being well–known examples, and demand employees with new skills.

KEY POINT The UK government and the EU have passed laws in an attempt to counter discrimination at work (see Chapter 4).

The mobility of labour

AQA A   AQA B
EDEXCEL
OCR A   OCR B
WJEC
NICCEA

In trying to solve the problem of unemployment, one option is to **move work to the workers**, e.g. by the government using policies to help regions that face special difficulties. The other option is to get **workers to move to the work**, by moving **area** or by changing **occupation**.

Jobless rate at 25-year low

Jobs boost for town as company moves on

Jobs are safe in sell-offs

Charity making workers jobless

Vauxhall axes 2,000

BA to shed 1,000 jobs at Gatwick

ICL warns of more jobs to go

Barclays cuts more jobs

Fig. 1.11 Ups and downs of the jobs market

Occupational mobility of labour

If people cannot or will not move areas to work, it may be possible for them to retrain, change career and find work where they are living. This can again prove difficult due to:

1. **ability** – an individual may not have the ability or skill to do certain work
2. **training** – people may regard themselves as too old to retrain, facilities for training may not be available, or retraining may be regarded as taking too long
3. **pay levels** – training or starting pay may be too low to attract people

Geographical mobility of labour

This occurs when people move from one area to another to get work. There are three main factors that may discourage a person from doing this.

> The high cost of living in a region is a particular problem if the jobs there don't carry a high wage (e.g. many service sector jobs are low paid).

1. **Family ties** – e.g. having children at school or relatives in the area where the person now lives.
2. **Costs** – e.g. the high cost of housing in London and the South-East means that many people can't afford to move there to work.
3. **Prejudice** – e.g. people may not be prepared to live and work in certain parts of the country.

Regional factors

Many changes have taken place in the various regions of the country in recent years. For example, the discovery of North Sea oil – as well as helping the UK economy in general – started a boom in the economy of Aberdeen and its surrounding area.

One key trend has been **regional deindustrialisation**, with the 1980s and 1990s seeing a reduction in the importance of our traditional heavy engineering and manufacturing industries which were based in certain parts of the country. As a result, unemployment in these areas grew rapidly, and many towns and cities in these regions suffered from 'inner-city decay'.

Therefore, central and local government, with the EU, adopted a range of **regional policies**. If workers will not go to the work, governments can adopt policies to encourage work to go to the workers. Firms have been encouraged to move to areas such as South Wales by being offered various incentives, because these areas qualify for government assistance (see Fig. 1.12). There are

■ Tier 1
■ Tier 2

Fig. 1.12 Areas qualifying for assistance (Source: DTI)

four 'Tier 1' areas identified on the map by : Cornwall, Merseyside, South Yorkshire, and West Wales and the Valleys of South Wales. Other government and EU support is available for the 'Tier 2' areas, shown on the map in ▮ .

> **KEY POINT**
> Even the more prosperous areas of the country, such as South-East England, have regional problems of traffic congestion and the high cost of living, which discourage people from moving there.

Other policies include:

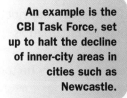
An example is the CBI Task Force, set up to halt the decline of inner-city areas in cities such as Newcastle.

● the DTI's **Phoenix Fund**, which encourages entrepreneurs in disadvantaged areas, and its **Regional Selective Assistance** scheme that attracts investment and jobs to the Assisted Areas by offering grants
● **Enterprise Grants**, giving financial help to small and medium-sized enterprises investing in projects in the Assisted Areas
● finance from the European Union through its **Social Fund**, to help improve road systems and reduce congestion
● initiatives by non-government organisations

> **PROGRESS CHECK**
>
> 1. How does the change in the age profile in the UK affect firms?
> 2. Match the following descriptions with the unemployment terms they represent:
>
> | | |
> |---|---|
> | (a) frictional | (i) lack of demand in the economy |
> | (b) structural | (ii) when people change jobs |
> | (c) seasonal | (iii) long-term changes in demand or supply |
> | (d) cyclical | (iv) machines substituted for labour |
> | (e) technological | (v) changes in demand at certain times of the year |
>
> 1. It may affect demand for their products, and the supply of their labour.
> 2. (a) with (ii); (b) with (iii); (c) with (v); (d) with (i); (e) with (iv).

1.4 *The location of industry*

After studying this section you should be able to understand:

● **historical and modern-day influences on location**
● **how the government influences location**

Influences on location

AQA A   AQA B
EDEXCEL
OCR A   OCR B
WJEC
NICCEA

Many factors influence where a firm is located. Fig. 1.13 shows the various 'pulls' on a firm.

These factors change in importance over time, for example because quality modern-day transport and communications systems have developed, and fuel and power sources have changed.

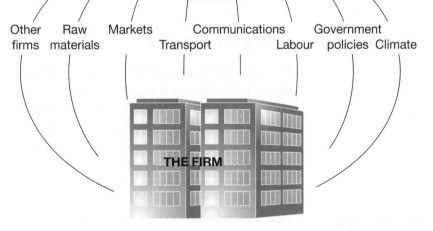

Other   Raw   Markets   Communications   Government
firms materials   Transport   Labour   policies Climate

THE FIRM

Fig. 1.13 Influences on where a firm locates

Historical factors

Many industries originally grew up near to the **supply of their raw materials**, such as the china industry in the Potteries area of Staffordshire. Other firms had to be based by **fuel or power supplies**, such as in a coal-mining area, because of the high cost of transporting the fuel. The availability of water and an appropriate climate, were important **natural advantages** in establishing the cotton and woollen industries that once flourished in the North of England. These factors are all less important nowadays, due to improved and cheaper methods of transport and the national availability of modern forms of power, although good climate and soil will always help decide whether an area is used for agriculture.

Modern-day influences

- Location near an efficient **transport network** has always been a major influence. In the past, canals and railways were influential forms of transport; today, being close to motorway networks, airports and seaports is important when deciding a firm's location.
- The entrepreneur will be tempted to locate the firm where there is an available and adequately skilled **labour force**. Certain areas of the country may contain people having particular knowledge and skills, such as in the Potteries area around Stoke-on-Trent, and in the Midlands with its car industry. The existence of these **external economies** (page 149) encourages new firms to set up in these areas.
- As a general rule, if a firm's raw materials are bulky and costly to transport, it will want to be located near the **source of its materials**. If it is in a 'weight-gaining' industry (e.g. brewing, where water is added to the raw ingredients) it will locate near the **market** for the finished product in order to save the high cost of transporting the finished goods.
- The **population** distribution is another influence. Firms producing consumer goods may be tempted to locate near areas of high population such as South-East England, although the high **cost of land** may discourage them.
- When it comes to locating a business, the owners will have their own likes and dislikes. This **personal choice** will be influenced by the personal 'ties' of the entrepreneur.

> Certain firms, mainly in the service sector, with local demand will have to be located close to their customers.

> **KEY POINT**
> The most important factor is how each of these influences affects the **cost** of locating.

The government

Central government has become an increasingly important influence in helping decide where firms are located. New towns such as Telford and Milton Keynes have been built, and **financial incentives** offered to business people to move to these areas. We already know from page 22 that the government offers incentives to encourage firms to set up in some regions of the country, particularly those regions suffering from high levels of unemployment due to the collapse of their traditional industries (e.g. shipbuilding and mining in North-East England). The **European Union** (page 63) also has a regional policy that seeks to help disadvantaged regions.

Central government has also played a more direct part in locating industry by setting up its own departments in areas with economic problems.

> Examples include the DVLC vehicle licensing centre in Swansea, and National Girobank plc in Bootle, Liverpool.

> **PROGRESS CHECK**
>
> 1. If an entrepreneur wishes to set up business in the UK, what factors influence where the new firm will be located?
>
> 1. Climate (agriculture); transport and communication systems; labour supply and skills; closeness of markets; external economies of scale; government influences.

1.5 **International trade**

LEARNING SUMMARY

After studying this section you should be able to understand:

● *the benefits to the UK of international trade*
● *how international trade may be restricted*
● *the UK's Balance of Payments*

The UK and international trade

AQA A   AQA B
EDEXCEL
OCR A   OCR B
WJEC
NICCEA

We may not be able to produce some products (e.g. tropical fruit), or may choose not to do so (an opportunity cost: page 10).

We know that countries **specialise** (page 10) in certain products. **Surpluses** are created through the UK specialising, which we can then **trade** with other countries in return for the goods and services we need. The UK, like all countries, depends on foreign trade for its survival.

The benefits from international trade

EXPORTS
Supply foreign currency
Create employment

IMPORTS
Bring customer choice
Supply items we need

THE UK

Fig. 1.14 Why we trade

- **Greater competition**. Importing goods and services from abroad provides home-based producers with competition they otherwise wouldn't have. This competition should lead to **lower prices** for consumers, and help guard against monopolies being created in the home country. The home-based producers themselves have **larger markets** through being able to export their products: this should result in higher production, with savings being passed on to the consumer.
- **Greater specialisation**. Countries can build up specialist expertise in particular goods and services. The UK, for example, has specialist financial services and telecommunications industries; other examples are Japan, which is noted for its electronic goods, and Denmark, for its foodstuffs. Specialisation should lead to **greater efficiency** and **higher output**.
- **Greater choice**. Differences in climate and natural resources mean that, if international trade didn't take place, some goods would never be available in the UK. There is also a wider choice of the goods and services that are available to us: for example, French, German and Italian vehicle manufacturers provide UK consumers with alternatives to home-built cars.

Why, then, does the UK trade? In addition to the advantages we've just met, an important result of higher output is **higher employment**, not only for labour but for all the factors of production (page 9). Also, we need **foreign currency** to buy what we can't or won't produce ourselves, and we obtain this foreign currency by selling our exports.

> **KEY POINT**   All countries gain from international trade bringing greater competition, **greater** specialisation and **greater** choice.

Problems of exporting

Problems include:

- differences in **measurements** – different weights, sizes and electrical voltages
- **language** difficulties – problems of communicating by letter or email, designing sales brochures and packaging, advertising etc.
- differences in **culture** – what may be acceptable or 'normal' in the UK may not be acceptable in certain other countries, for example for religious reasons
- **trading risks** – the risk of granting credit to new overseas clients
- **payment** – the overseas client may pay in foreign currency, which has to be converted to sterling
- **costs** – higher transport and insurance costs compared with selling in the home market
- **import restrictions** – a country may set restrictions (page 27) on goods that can be imported
- **documentation** – in non-EU countries there can be complicated procedures that the exporting firm has to follow

For example, white is the colour of mourning in Japan and green in Singapore, which affects how we package and what we sell to these countries.

Restrictions on international trade

AQA A   AQA B
EDEXCEL
OCR A   OCR B
WJEC
NICCEA

A government may take action to restrict international trade. For example, it may decide to restrict imports into a country for a number of reasons. Restricting international trade by using tariffs (see below) can **raise revenue**; the government may seek to **protect existing industries** from competition, and to **protect 'infant industries'** that are not yet fully established; it may also wish to **restrict 'dumping'** of foreign goods (goods that are being exported at extremely low prices by countries wishing to establish a market).

The following are the main types of action normally taken.

- **Tariffs** are import duties, such as the customs and excise duties of the UK, which can be an important source of government revenue. Tariffs **raise the price** of the imported item, making it less competitive.
- **Quotas** are physical restrictions on the **amount** of an item that can be imported: for example, the UK government set a limit on the number of Japanese cars that could be imported.
- **Subsidies** are given to **home producers**, which make their goods cheaper and therefore more competitive than those from importers.
- **Embargoes** are **bans on importing** certain items, e.g. for political reasons.

 KEY POINT — The main disadvantage to a country restricting international trade is that other countries 'follow suit', with the risk of a trade war and an economic recession.

The UK's balance of payments

AQA A   AQA B
EDEXCEL
OCR A   OCR B
WJEC
NICCEA

Until recently, we were regarded as a producer of manufactured goods for export, with raw materials and foodstuffs being imported in return. Although exports of manufactured goods are still important, as we can see below in Fig. 1.15, the largest imports to the UK are now also finished manufactured goods.

Product	Exports (£ million)	Imports (£ million)
Food and beverages	10 302	17 080
Fuel and crude materials	9 283	10 334
Chemicals	22 311	18 145
Manufactured goods	121 489	143 398

Fig. 1.15 The UK's main exports and imports (1998) (Source: ONS)

There are several reasons for the change in our imports and exports.

- The growth of the manufacturing sector in other countries and areas such as the Far East has led to **increased competition**.
- **Lower costs** may exist in competing countries, e.g. in wages, making their exported goods cheaper than our home-produced ones.
- In some areas we may have a **less efficient management and workforce** than other competing countries, e.g. due to a lack of investment in up-to-date technology. The result is that some UK-manufactured products may be of **poor design and quality**.

The Balance of Trade

The Balance of Payments records the inflow and outflow of our foreign currency as a result of exporting and importing our goods and services. The Balance of Payments is made up of the import and export of '**visibles**' and '**invisibles**'. We calculate the Balance of Trade, or 'visible balance', in this way:

visible exports
less visible imports
= balance of trade

In June 2000, for example, the UK had a trading deficit with the rest of the EU of £740 million, and a £2.1 billion deficit with the rest of the world.

Visible exports and imports are of **goods only**, and don't include services. If visible exports are greater than visible imports, there is a **surplus** on our country's balance of trade: if visible imports are greater, there is a **deficit**. Fig. 1.16 shows that in recent years the UK has had a substantial deficit in 'visibles'.

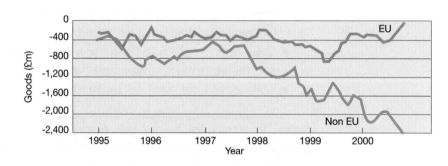

Fig. 1.16 Britain's trading gap with the rest of the world (Source: ONS)

The Balance of Payments

The Balance of Payments includes the information from the Balance of Trade, and also takes into account '**invisibles**', the export and import of services. A country's balance of payments may be **favourable** or **adverse** (unfavourable). Fig. 1.17 illustrates the UK's balance of payments.

Balance of Payments

	Current account (£ million)		International investment (£ million)	
Trade in goods	–20 765		Investment abroad	110.6
Trade in services	12 253		Investment in the UK	–95.5
Total trade	–8 512		Net earnings from investment	15.1
Other adjustments	8 648			
Current balance	136			

Fig. 1.17 The UK's balance of payments, 1998 (Source: ONS)

PROGRESS CHECK

1. Three benefits from international trade are greater _____ , greater _____ and greater _____ .
2. Explain the difference between the Balance of Trade and the Balance of Payments.

2. Trade is 'visibles' (goods) only; Payments includes both 'visibles' and 'invisibles'.
1. Choice; specialisation; competition.

Sample GCSE questions

This question is based on location of industry.

1. Gochetts Ltd. has been manufacturing electrical components used in washing machines and other household goods for over 40 years. Its factory, located on a dockside site, is now due for redevelopment into a marina and other leisure facilities. The particular site on which the factory stood has recently been bought by a large hotel company and it is planning to build a luxury hotel on the site. Gotchetts Ltd. will use the money obtained from selling their old factory to build on a new site on the outskirts of the town.

(a) Suggest and explain **three** factors the directors of Gotchetts Ltd. will need to consider in trying to find a new site. **(6)**

> *Firstly the company will have to consider the cost of the site - how much it will cost them to stay there. Secondly, the company needs to check how easy it will be for the present workforce to get to the new site, because they won't want to lose staff. Lastly, the company needs to check how easy it will be for lorries and other transport to get to and from the new site.*

'Cost' is perhaps the most important factor, but you should state the cost of something (e.g. in this case, the cost of buying the land). Also include the knock–on cost of having to recruit new staff.

(b) Consider the disadvantages for Gotchetts Ltd. of moving to a new site. **(6)**

> *It will cause everybody a lot of upheaval, so the company will have to take this into account. It will interrupt production, which could be a real problem if there are lots of orders to meet. The company will have to tell its customers where it is. Its suppliers will also have to be told.*

'Everybody' is unclear (it's better to give examples such as employees, managers and directors). The points could have been developed, e.g. by describing problems of not being able to meet orders (loss of income, loss of goodwill, loss of future custom) and thinking about communication, e.g. the need to redesign and reprint stationery.

(c) Evaluate the likely impact of the proposed move on the local community. **(8)**

> *The local community will be gaining a nicer area, because they will prefer a marina and leisure facilities to having a factory on their doorstep. The traffic may change, from lorries delivering and collecting electrical components to cars and taxis delivering and collecting people stopping at the hotel and going to the marina. This could be better or worse, depending on the transport links. The local community may gain more jobs. Assuming they can get to where Gotchetts Ltd. is moving to, the existing people working there can go with Gotchetts, while the unemployed people living there may have a chance of working in the new marina, hotel and leisure facilities.*

You could also mention the likely rise in price of their homes if a 'nicer' living area is being created. 'Infrastructure' is a good word to use to describe the transport network. You should also consider the other major social costs or benefits, such as noise (perhaps less during the day but more at night) and pollution (probably less, although possibly more traffic).

WJEC Foundation Tier, June 2000

Exam practice questions

This is a question on how a firm is affected by changes in the local population.

1. Hadleigh Sports and Leisure Centre is based in a town of approximately 80 000 people. This population is expected to increase by about 5% in the next 10 years, and to have a changed age profile as shown below:

Age group	At present (%)	In 10 years (%)
65 and over	17	25
46–64	23	29
26–45	6	22
16–25	15	8
Under 16	19	16

(a) Analyse how these expected changes in age structure could affect the Centre's market. (8)

....

....

....

....

....

....

....

(b) Explain how the Centre might react to these changes. (4)

....

....

....

....

2 Business organisations

The following topics are included in this chapter:

- **The private sector**
- **Sole traders and partnerships**
- **Limited companies**
- **Other forms of private sector organisation**
- **The public sector**
- **Stakeholders**

2.1 The private sector

LEARNING SUMMARY

After studying this section you should be able to understand:

- **the structure of the UK's economy**
- **the main objectives of firms**
- **the difference between unincorporated and incorporated business**

The UK's economy

AQA A   AQA B
EDEXCEL
OCR A   OCR B
WJEC
NICCEA

The UK has a mixed economy, the 'mix' being made up of private sector and public sector organisations. The main organisations are shown in Fig. 2.1.

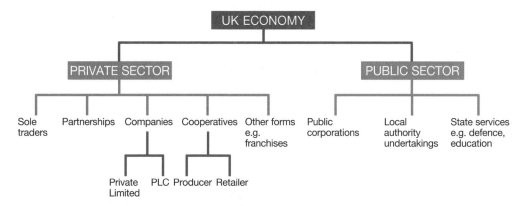

Fig. 2.1 Business organisations in the UK economy

- **Private sector firms** are owned by individuals, not by the State. The firms can be small or large, owned by one person or by thousands of people. By producing and selling their products, they make a **profit** for their owners.
- The **public sector** consists of both central government and local government organisations, the firms and industries in this sector **providing services** and being run mainly under State control.

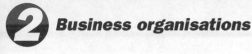

Features of the private sector

AQA A   AQA B
EDEXCEL
OCR A   OCR B
WJEC
NICCEA

Objectives of private sector firms

Firms that operate in the private sector have a series of objectives. Their owners will want them to **survive** in the very competitive world in which they operate. If losses are made in the short term, these may be accepted in the hope that business will improve in the future.

Entrepreneurs – the 'risk taker' businessmen and businesswomen – may also set an objective to gain a larger share of their local, national or international market. One way they may try to get this **larger market share** is to cut their prices, and so be willing (again for a short time) to accept lower profits, or even losses, to achieve this objective.

Growth is an objective closely linked to market share, and to survival. Larger firms are more likely to survive, e.g. by gaining from economies of scale (page 148), and they have more control of the prices they charge and of their market in general.

> The entrepreneur may also have a personal desire to see the firm grow in size.

These entrepreneurs are really in this sector to make a profit. This **profit motive** encourages people either to invest in existing firms – by buying their shares on the stock market, for example – or to establish themselves in business, perhaps on their own or in partnership with a colleague. By growing and increasing its market share, the firm is more likely to make acceptable profits for its owners.

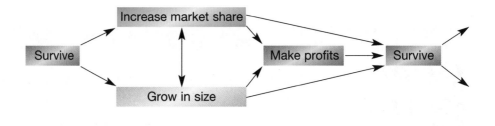

Fig. 2.2 The main objectives in the private sector

> **KEY POINT**
> There are close links between these business objectives: they are interrelated.

Unincorporated and incorporated businesses

A typical example of a **sole trader** is the traditional corner shop, selling groceries, newspapers, sweets and tobacco, and likely to be owned by the person serving in the shop. We see examples of **partnerships** in the main streets of towns and villages: the 'professions', such as doctors and dentists, accountants and lawyers, are often run as partnerships. **Limited companies** are also widely found in the three sectors of our economy, particularly in the secondary (manufacturing and construction) and tertiary (e.g. retailing) sectors.

> Boots, Sainsbury's and Marks & Spencer are good examples of the 'household name' limited companies.

Sole traders and partnerships are **unincorporated** businesses. The effects of a business being unincorporated are that:

● there is **no separate legal existence** from its owners – this means that these firms can't enter contracts in their own names, and the owners are fully responsible for the business debts
● sole traders and partners have **unlimited liability** for these business debts
● there are **few formalities** necessary to set up in business, compared with setting up a limited company

Limited companies are examples of **incorporated** businesses. Unlike sole traders and partnership firms, limited companies have **more formalities** to go through before being established. Another important difference is that limited companies have a **separate legal existence** from their owners (their shareholders). This means that a limited company can **take legal action in its own name**, and that the owners are not personally responsible for the business debts: they have **limited liability**.

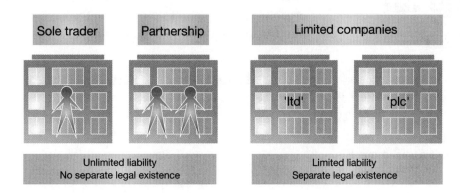
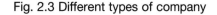

Fig. 2.3 Different types of company

The advantages of limited liability

If we have money to invest, we'll find there are many investment options from which to choose. One may be to set up in business as a sole proprietor in the hope of making profits: another is to invest the money in an existing limited company.

Limited liability encourages people to invest, because they know there's a limit to the amount of money they can lose.

If our sole trader business fails, as well as losing the money invested, we may also be forced to **use personal savings to meet business debts**. If the limited company is 'wound up', however, we only lose what we've invested in the company, and no more. **Our liability is limited** to the value we've invested (or which we've agreed to invest, if we haven't paid it all yet).

KEY POINT

A limited company must use 'Ltd.' or 'plc' in its name, to warn those trading with it that its liability is limited, and so they may not be able to recover what they're owed if the company can't meet these debts itself.

PROGRESS CHECK

1. State **four** main objectives of firms in the private sector.
2. What are the **two** key differences between unincorporated and incorporated businesses?

1. Survival; growth; increased market share; profit. 2. Legal existence; limitation of liability.

2.2 Sole traders and partnerships

LEARNING SUMMARY

After studying this section you should be able to understand:

● *sole traders*
● *partnerships*

Sole traders

AQA A   AQA B
EDEXCEL
OCR A   OCR B
WJEC
NICCEA

Also known as **sole proprietors**, these are the most commonly found type of business in the UK. They are owned and controlled by one person, who has to organise (and sometimes provide) all the capital required. Formation is easy, and the structure of the firm is usually simple.

> Many sole traders provide specialist services, such as plumbers, carpenters and hairdressers: they meet a local demand for their product.

Advantages and disadvantages of being a sole trader

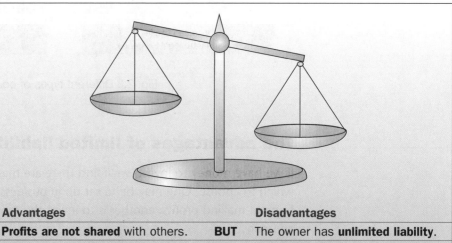

> The Small Firms Loan Guarantee scheme of the DTI (page 72) guarantees loans for small businesses which can't get a loan due to a lack of security.

Advantages		Disadvantages
Profits are not shared with others.	**BUT**	The owner has **unlimited liability**.
The firm is usually small-scale, so **small amounts of capital** are needed.	**BUT**	Its small-scale nature makes it **difficult to expand**.
The owner is his or her **own boss**.	**BUT**	**Responsibility can't easily be shared.**
Quick decisions can be made.	**BUT**	**Long hours** and **few holidays** are typical.
The business is **easy to establish**.	**BUT**	It can be **difficult to continue** if the owner dies or retires.

Fig. 2.4 Advantages and disadvantages of being a sole trader

> **KEY POINT**
>
> Sole traders can still employ people to work for them: it's the **ownership** that's limited to one person.

Partnerships

AQA A   AQA B
EDEXCEL
OCR A   OCR B
WJEC
NICCEA

Partnerships are also easily formed. The partners usually draw up a **deed of partnership** (a partnership **agreement**) setting out the key details.

> **AGREEMENT**
> Names of partners ....
> Capital contributed £ ....
> £ ....
> How profits and losses are shared ....
> Partnership salary: £ ....
> paid to ....

Fig. 2.5 Content of partnership agreement

If the partners haven't drawn up an agreement, the **1890 Partnership Act** lays down some rules. The partners share profits and losses equally, they are not entitled to a salary, nor do they receive any interest on the capital they've invested, but any loans they make to the partnership receive 5% interest per annum.

Partnerships can be formed almost as easily as can sole trader businesses. When we compare them to the sole trader form, a partnership has a number of advantages.

1. Since there will be at least two partners, they can **divide control** of the business between them (however, **disputes** may arise between the partners).
2. Division of labour becomes possible, with partners being able to **specialise** in certain business functions.
3. Management and responsibility can be **shared** by the partners, allowing greater time off and more holidays than are possible for sole traders.
4. Partnerships tend to have **more capital** than sole traders, because there are more owners who can contribute. Expansion is therefore easier (though may still be difficult).
5. There is **greater continuity** than for a sole trader.

> **If a partner leaves the firm, or a new partner joins it, the existing partnership is technically ended and a new one starts.**

> **KEY POINT**   Like sole traders, partners still face unlimited liability.

The limited liability partnership (LLP)

> **It's likely that a number of large professional partnerships, such as accountants and lawyers, may decide to become LLPs.**

Partners in existing partnership had become more and more concerned with unlimited liability, and in 2000 the **Limited Liability Partnerships Act** was passed. This new form of business ownership is similar to a limited company, in that:

- the LLP is a **legal person** separate from its members
- it also has to use an abbreviation ('**LLP**') at the end of its name

PROGRESS CHECK

1. Identify **two** advantages and **two** disadvantages of a sole trader, compared with a partnership.

1. Advantages: sole trader doesn't have to share profit, and is in total control. Disadvantages: less capital normally available; cannot share responsibility as easily.

2.3 Limited companies

LEARNING SUMMARY

After studying this section you should be able to understand:

● *the main features of limited companies*
● *formation of a company*
● *the public and private forms of a limited company*

Features of limited companies

AQA A AQA B
EDEXCEL
OCR A OCR B
WJEC
NICCEA

We have two types of limited company: **public limited companies** – plcs – and **private limited companies** ('Ltd.'). The most important difference between these is that the shares (see page 99) of the plc are 'quoted' – in other words, their price is established, and they can be bought and sold – on the stock exchange to members of the public.

Both types of company can be formed by a minimum of two shareholders. We have already seen two key features:

1. there is **limited liability** – the liability of the shareholders is limited to the amount of their investment in the company
2. there is a **separate legal existence** – a limited company can, in its own name, sue and be sued, own property and other assets, and can enter into contracts

In addition, a limited company has **greater continuity**: its separate legal existence isn't affected by what happens to one of its shareholders. There is also a **separation of ownership from control** in these companies. Unlike partnerships and sole traders, where the owners usually run the business themselves, the owners – **shareholders** – of a limited company often have little say in the running of the company. It is the **directors**, elected by shareholders at the company's **AGM** (Annual General Meeting), who control the company. Policies are decided by the Board of Directors, and are carried out through **delegation** (page 51).

> In practice, the directors appoint managers to help them control the company.

Setting up a limited company

There are a number of steps to tasks in setting up a limited company. These are summarised in Fig. 2.6.

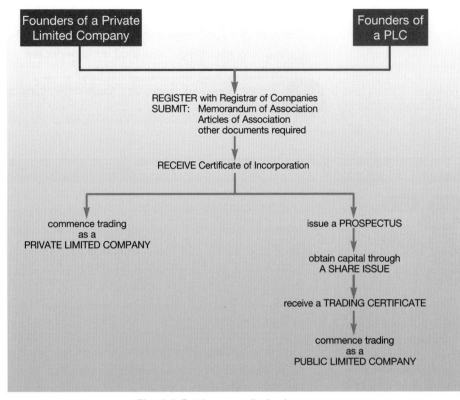

Fig. 2.6 Setting up a limited company

The two most important documents the company must produce are the memorandum of association and the articles of association.

Memorandum of Association	Articles of Association
Name	Directors
Objects	Meetings
Situation	Profits
Liability	
Capital	
Association	

Fig. 2.7 Memorandum of association and articles of association

The **memorandum of association** contains details of how the company relates to its **external world**. It contains a number of clauses:

- the **name** clause ensures it doesn't copy another company's name
- the **objects** clause explains the purpose for which it was set up (e.g. to make tyres, or to construct buildings)
- its **situation** clause states where its registered office is located
- the **liability** clause confirms that the members have limited liability
- the **capital** clause describes the amount and type of capital it will have
- the **association** clause must be signed by at least some of the people creating the company

The **articles of association** governs the **internal workings** of the company. The articles include how **directors** are elected, and the number, rights and duties; how **meetings** are called and conducted; and how **profits** are shared.

> **KEY POINT**
>
> Multinational companies (page 41) usually operate as plcs in the United Kingdom.

Private and public companies

AQA A AQA B
EDEXCEL
OCR A OCR B
WJEC
NICCEA

> Page 113, which contains Sainsbury's financial details, illustrates the information that plcs must 'make public'.

Although we refer to limited 'Ltd.' companies as 'private', their business affairs are less private than those of partnerships and sole traders. The directors have to get the company's accounts **audited** – checked by auditors for accuracy and truthfulness – and must disclose some financial information to the government (e.g. for tax purposes). Compared with a plc, however, the ordinary limited company is more private, because members of the public don't have access to its accounts.

The main advantage a plc has over a private limited company is that it can **raise capital from the public**. It does this by advertising its shares for sale. The other advantages it has tend to come from its **greater size**:

- it may benefit from **economies of scale** (page 148)
- it is **easier to borrow money** because of its size and the security it can offer
- through its size, a plc can more easily **specialise**, e.g. by using specialist equipment and employing specialist staff

Plcs also have some disadvantages. We already know that a plc's annual accounts are **open to public inspection** because they have to be published, and that formation of the company is **complicated and expensive**. Other possible drawbacks for plcs are:

- they may become **too large** and suffer from diseconomies of scale (page 150)
- ownership may change almost overnight, through **take-over bids** (page 59) being launched by rivals seeking to buy the plc's shares on the stock exchange
- the **directors' interests may differ from those of the shareholders**, because ownership and control have become separate
- the plc may be dominated by a few shareholders, e.g. by **institutional investors** such as pension funds and insurance companies

> For example, the directors may have long-term plans to get a larger market share, but the shareholders may want immediate and large profits.

Fig. 2.8 Takeovers make the news

1. State the main difference between a plc and a private company.
2. Explain the difference between the memorandum and the articles of association.

2. Memorandum governs the relationship with the outside world; articles explain the internal relationships.
1. A plc can apply to the public for share capital; ltd company cannot.

2.4 Other forms of private sector organisation

After studying this section you should be able to understand:

- *co-operatives*
- *franchisors and franchisees*
- *multinational companies*

Co-operatives

AQA A AQA B
EDEXCEL
OCR A OCR B
WJEC
NICCEA

> **Popular areas for setting up new worker co-operatives include printing, publishing and design; foodstuffs; engineering and general manufacture; and textiles and fashion.**

We have two main forms of co-operative in the UK economy: **worker** (or **producer**) co-operatives, and **retail** co-operatives.

Worker co-operatives

These vary in size and in organisation. In the UK, they have sometimes been formed by groups of workers **buying out** their company, which may have been troubled by financial or trading problems. In worker co-operatives, the members contribute the capital and share the profits, usually running the co-operative on democratic lines. Some specialists, such as accountants, may have to be employed.

Retail co-operatives

Started by the 'Rochdale Pioneers' in 1844 because they were being exploited by local shops, the '**Co-op**' is a well-known retail outlet in many towns. These Co-operative Retail Societies (CRS) have the following features:

- **wider aims** than most other business organisations – for example, more far-reaching political, social and ethical aims
- **anyone can join** a Society by buying a share in it (these shares aren't traded on the stock exchange)
- there is **one vote per member** regardless of the number of shares held
- **members share the profits** and **elect the management committee**

Individual retail co-operatives are supplied by the **CWS** – the Co-operative Wholesale Society – which allows them to take advantage of bulk-buying economies. The CWS employs over 50 000 people, and its annual sales make it the world's largest retail-linked co-operative. Its specialist areas include travel, funerals and garages, and it is one of Britain's biggest farmers.

Franchising agreements

AQA A   AQA B
EDEXCEL
OCR A   OCR B
WJEC
NICCEA

Well-known franchises include Prontaprint, Kentucky Fried Chicken and Thrifty Car Rental.

In 1977 eight firms, including the fast-food chain Wimpy, launched the **British Franchise Association** (BFA). There are currently about 600 business franchises in the UK, comprising about 30 000 franchisees.

Franchising involves a company – the **franchisor** – allowing its **franchisees** (people who have bought the franchise) to use its logo and sell its products.

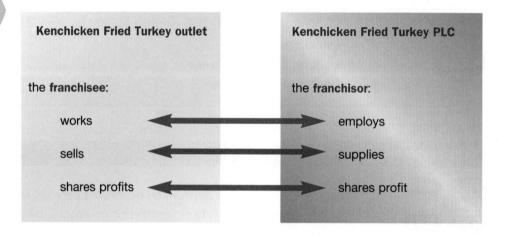

Fig. 2.9 A typical franchise relationship

Franchising **reduces the risk of business failure** because the franchisee is supported by the successful business record of the franchisor.

Main benefits to the franchisee	Main benefits to the franchisor
a recognised product	expansion without having to invest the capital
specialist support and advice	highly motivated franchisees

'Franchisees' backgrounds are diverse, as we select on a broad range of business skills ... The overall fee will comprise an initial lump sum plus a royalty based upon turnover ... almost all of the equipment that you would require in your business is available on finance agreements ... Before joining the Network you will have completed a comprehensive induction training programme with an existing franchisee ...'

Fig. 2.10 How ANC, the franchised express parcel carrier, explains its franchise arrangement (Source: ANC 1999)

Multinational companies

A multinational company is one that **produces in more than one country**. However, its ownership is based in a single country: for example, it may operate as a **holding company** (a company that 'holds' overall control of its different companies, which then do business in their own names).

> Multinationals are responsible for over a third of the world's total production.

> Four years ago we became the leader in a market of 59 million – the UK. We now operate in eight countries with a combined population of nearly 250 million, providing a large base for additional sales and profit growth in the future ... We now employ over 200,000 people world-wide ... We now have 821 stores world-wide ...

Fig. 2.11 Tesco as a multinational (Source: Tesco plc Annual Review and Summary Financial Statement 1999)

The effect of multinationals on the UK's economy

They bring many benefits to our economy:

- **reduction of unemployment** – e.g. Nissan starting production in North-east England and Toyota in the Midlands, both regions having been badly hit by unemployment
- **introduction of new technology** – the presence of these two car companies in the UK encouraged other car manufacturers to adopt more up-to-date equipment and processes
- **training in up-to-date skills** – multinationals often provide efficient training schemes, or may link up with other training providers to improve the skills of the local workforce
- **other benefits** – including providing work for local suppliers of the components and services that these multinationals need

There are disadvantages to the UK and other countries associated with multinational operations. The following are typical problems that can arise:

- the multinational may **import expertise** of its own, bringing in managers and trained staff rather than recruiting locally
- it may introduce its own work practices, which can lead to **industrial disputes**
- it can **send profits out of the country**, to its 'home' country
- there may be **problems of control** – because of their size and power, multinational companies can exert great influence on a government's economic policies

PROGRESS CHECK

1. (a) Name the **two** forms of co-operative organisation.
   (b) Name the **two** parties to a franchise agreement.
2. Identify **one** benefit and **one** drawback of allowing multinationals to operate in the UK economy.

2. Benefit: increased employment. Drawback: exporting its profits.
1. (a) Worker co-operatives; retailer co-operatives. (b) Franchisor; franchisee

2.5 The public sector

LEARNING SUMMARY

After studying this section you should be able to understand:

● *why organisations are publicly owned*
● *the types of public sector organisation*

Reasons for public ownership

AQA A   AQA B
EDEXCEL
OCR A   OCR B
WJEC
NICCEA

The public sector of the economy consists of those firms and industries for which **central or local government** is mainly responsible. These are **paid for through the taxation system**, and their purpose is to **provide services for the whole population**.

SECTOR OF THE ECONOMY	OWNERSHIP	SOURCES OF FINANCE	REASON FOR EXISTENCE
PRIVATE SECTOR	**PRIVATE INDIVIDUALS**	**INDIVIDUALS AND FIRMS**	**PROFIT MOTIVE**
Sole traders	One person	Sole trader	Profit for owner
Partnerships	Two or more individuals	Partners	Profit for partners
Limited companies	Two or more shareholders	Shareholders	Profit for shareholders
		Other sources, e.g. commercial banks	
PUBLIC SECTOR	**CENTRAL & LOCAL GOVERNMENT**	**PUBLIC FUNDS**	**SERVICE MOTIVE**
Public corporations	Central government	Taxation and trading	To provide a service, and break even or make profit
Local authority undertakings	Local government	Local finance and trading	To provide a service, and break even or make profit

Fig. 2.12 Private and public sectors: the main differences

This sector includes activities such as State education, the National Health Service, and the armed forces.

Arguments for and against public ownership

The government may decide to take a firm or an industry into public ownership for a number of reasons:

1. to **control a 'natural monopoly'**, e.g. to ensure that water is safely purified and distributed
2. to **take control of a private sector monopoly** which could otherwise exploit people
3. to make sure that **unprofitable but essential services** are provided (e.g. health, waste disposal)
4. to **protect an industry**, and therefore protect jobs
5. to **ensure national security** by controlling defence
6. to **provide capital for large-scale developments**

Public ownership brings with it some disadvantages, however. It can lead to problems of **inefficiency**, since there may be no competition and little incentive to improve efficiency. **Diseconomies of scale** can also occur due to the size of the organisations. **Losses** normally have to be met out of taxation, and **political interference** in the organisations may also take place.

Types of public sector organisations

AQA A   AQA B
EDEXCEL
OCR A   OCR B
WJEC
NICCEA

Public corporations and nationalised industries

A public corporation is formed by an **Act of Parliament**, which sets up the corporation's functions and organisation. Its day-to-day policy is decided by its board, appointed by a government minister, and the government sets its financial targets.

KEY POINT A public corporation is quite different from a public limited company.

Other public corporations still in the public sector have been affected by deregulation, which allows greater competition to take place, or by using private sector services where these services are cheaper.

REVAMP FOR POST OFFICES

Row over plans for new Post Office plc

Delivery for Post Office
But there is a price for the commercial freedom

Fig. 2.13 The Post Office debate: public or private?

During the 1980s and 1990s many public corporations and nationalised industries were **privatised** by the government: this means they were **transferred from the public sector to the private sector**, becoming plcs. The belief was that, by doing so, these organisations would **become more efficient** through greater competition.

Primary sector	Secondary sector	Tertiary sector
British Coal	British Aerospace	British Railways
British Petroleum	British Steel	British Airways
	Rolls Royce	

Fig. 2.14 Some of the major privatisations in the UK

Local authority undertakings

Also known as 'municipal undertakings', these are businesses operated by the local authority on a commercial basis. The **finance** for their operation is raised locally, and they **receive income** from selling their services. Any **profits** made can be 'ploughed back' to improve and expand the services offered.

PROGRESS CHECK

1. Distinguish between a public company and a public corporation.
2. Identify **one** advantage and **one** disadvantage associated with public ownership.

1. A public company (plc) seeks to make profits in the private sector; a public corporation is a State-owned organisation providing a service for the general public.
2. Advantage: ensures that unprofitable but essential services are provided. Disadvantage: lack of competition may lead to inefficiency.

2.6 Stakeholders

LEARNING SUMMARY

After studying this section you should be able to understand:
- *the types of stakeholders*
- *the effect of stakeholders on an organisation*

Stakeholders in the economy

AQA A   AQA B
EDEXCEL
OCR A   OCR B
WJEC
NICCEA

Stakeholders are groups of people who have an **interest in**, and an **influence on**, an organisation. Figure 2.15 shows us that some stakeholders are **internal** to the firm, and others are **external** to it.

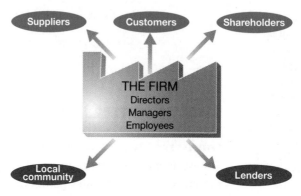

Fig. 2.15 Internal and external stakeholders

The influence of stakeholders

AQA A   AQA B
EDEXCEL
OCR A   OCR B
WJEC
NICCEA

Shell companies recognise five areas of responsibility:

1   to shareholders
2   to customers
3   to employees
4   to those with whom they do business
5   to society

Fig. 2.16 Shell's view of its stakeholders (Source: Royal Dutch/Shell Group of Companies, 1997)

There will also be clashes between different stakeholder groups in the public sector.

Stakeholders are particularly influential in the private sector. Here, the organisation's directors have important obligations to their shareholders (who elect them in the first place). These obligations normally include making an acceptable amount of profit, to keep the shareholders happy. The **profit motive** may, however, clash with the interests of other stakeholders. For example:

● customers may want lower prices, which would eat into the firm's profit margin and affect its profits
● the firm's suppliers and lenders are more interested in its **financial stability**, and less concerned with whether it is making high short-term profits
● its employees are more interested in job security than short-term profit performance

KEY POINT

There may be conflict between any of these stakeholder groups, because they tend to be interested in different aspects and objectives of the firm, and hold different opinions on how important each of the firm's objectives is.

PROGRESS CHECK

1. Name **two** internal, and **two** external, stakeholder groups in the private sector.

1. Internal: directors and employees. External: lenders and the local community.

Sample GCSE questions

This question is about business objectives, and forms of business organisation.

1. EV plc is a company selling printing franchises. Its directors have two main business objectives, increasing profit and increasing market share.

This is a good start, explaining briefly the terms used in the question.

(a) Explain how EV plc's objectives may be linked. **(4)**

> *'Profit' is what a company like EV makes when its revenue is greater than its expenses. Market share is EV's share of the market for printing. If EV is making good profits, it can use them to expand its market share. It does this by putting the profits into the company.*

Again a relevant and accurate point: you could rephrase 'putting the profits into the company' as 'retaining the profits', and add the point that the company uses the cash kept in the company to help it expand, and therefore increase market share.

EV plc is also looking for people to take on franchises in their printing business. Laura Lloyd, who already runs her own printing shop as a sole trader, has seen the advertisement and is considering taking on a franchise. The other alternative Laura has considered is to go into partnership with her sister, Emily.

(b) Advise Laura whether she should take on the franchise. **(6)**

> *Laura gains from having EV's product which is probably well known and could be national. She can use EV's expertise as well. The company will provide her with the advice and help she may need.*

Good points, but probably more relevant if Laura didn't already know how to run her business. You need to explain the drawbacks to Laura, e.g. loss of independence and having to pay the company out of her profits (or a royalty from her sales).

(c) Explain **one** benefit and **one** drawback to Laura from remaining a sole trader rather than going into partnership with her sister. **(6)**

> *Laura keeps her independence: she doesn't have to take Emily's views into account. But if she did go into partnership, she would have to ask Emily about business decisions.*

These are accurate points, though they could have been made more clearly. Explain that the first point, a benefit of staying a sole trader, is you are your own boss through this independence (and so, for example, you keep all the profits). The second point is also an advantage (shared responsibility and decision-making), so explain the 'downside' of having to take someone else's views into consideration.

(d) Give **two** reasons why companies such as EV plc prefer to expand by franchising rather than through opening their own shops. **(4)**

> *EV doesn't have to find the capital to invest, because Laura and the other franchisees will pay it. Secondly, EV doesn't have to take on the full responsibility of running the shops and so on.*

Well explained: instead of 'and so on', you could give a further example such as having to find and appoint staff.

Exam practice questions

Here are two questions on forms of business ownership.

1. Which **three** of the following statements apply to public limited companies? **(3)**

    N.B. Do not tick more than **three** boxes.

    The name of the company is ☐ The name of the company is ☐
    followed by the letters 'plc' followed by the letters 'Ltd.'

    The maximum number of ☐ Shares are sold on the Stock Exchange ☐
    shareholders is 20

    Shares cannot be sold to members ☐ They have a minimum share capital ☐
    of the general public of £50 000

    They are owned by the government ☐ They have unlimited liability ☐
    on behalf of the public

    WJEC Specimen Paper 1

2. Below is a list of features of different types of businesses.
    Select the **four** which **usually** apply to general partnerships. **(4)**

    General partnerships usually:

    (a) are owned by one person
    (b) sell shares on the Stock Exchange
    (c) have the letters plc at the end of their names
    (d) have unlimited liability
    (e) are owned by shareholders but cannot sell shares to the general public
    (f) share responsibilities between the owners
    (g) do not have more than twenty owners
    (h) have limited liability
    (i) share the workload between the owners
    (j) pay dividends to their shareholders

    WJEC Paper 1, 2000

The structure of organisations

The following topics are included in this chapter:

- Internal organisation
- Communication in business
- The impact of change
- Size and growth

3.1 Internal organisation

LEARNING SUMMARY

After studying this section you should be able to understand:
- the main functions and departments of a typical business
- the role of organisation charts
- the terms used to describe and analyse organisations' structures

The main functions

AQA A AQA B
EDEXCEL
OCR A OCR B
WJEC
NICCEA

There is usually a link between an organisation's business **objectives** and its **internal structure**. Most firms in the private sector are organised by **function**. They divide their work into a series of key **departments**, which allows **specialisation** to take place. Specialist managers and staff, and specialist equipment, can be employed to increase output and improve efficiency. Some firms – often multinational companies – may be organised on a **product** basis, operating as a series of 'divisions' or groups.

KEY POINT   How a business is organised is influenced by its objectives.

The main departments

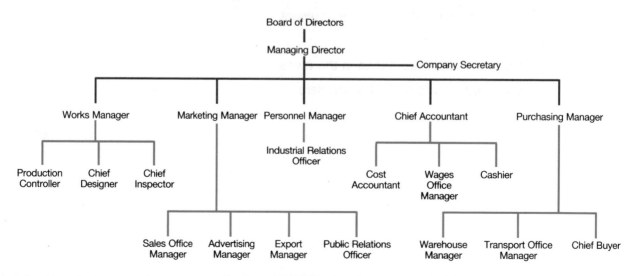

Fig. 3.1 The departments and structure of a typical manufacturing company

Firms 'produce' services as well as goods.

- **Production**. This is a vital department for manufacturing firms. It turns the raw material **inputs** into the finished goods **outputs**.
- **Accounting**. The accounting function – sometimes called the **finance** function – has the responsibility of obtaining, recording, controlling and analysing the firm's funds. Its efficient operation is vital to the firm's survival, e.g. by forecasting future cash flows to make sure there is enough cash to pay the debts the firm owes.
- **Marketing**. This function is responsible for activities such as selling, market research, packaging design, promotion (advertising), and distribution. It acts as the all-important link with the firm's customers.
- **Purchasing**. The **buying** function ensures that the firm gets the correct quantity and quality of raw materials and other items it requires, at the correct times.
- **Personnel**. This department is responsible for 'hiring and firing' of the staff who are working in the firm. It will keep staff records, organise their wages, and negotiate with them about pay and conditions of work.

The Personnel function is nowadays often called 'human resources'.

> **KEY POINT**
>
> These functions are interdependent: they link, and work closely, with each other.

Matrix structure

Many organisations have reduced the number of layers in their hierarchy, to make it 'flatter'. In doing so, they may take the emphasis away from the traditional functions and towards operations, projects, or tasks. This **matrix** structure focuses more on **achieving tasks**. Fig. 3.2 summarises the reorganised structure of the Bank of Scotland. This new structure is more operation-based by 'focusing strongly on the creation of products and services tailored to customers' needs'. The diagram shows 'Three strong customer-facing Divisions' that are supported by 'two internal centres of expertise'.

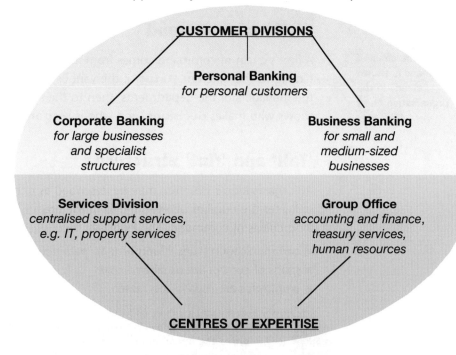

CUSTOMER DIVISIONS

Personal Banking
for personal customers

Corporate Banking
for large businesses and specialist structures

Business Banking
for small and medium-sized businesses

Services Division
centralised support services, e.g. IT, property services

Group Office
accounting and finance, treasury services, human resources

CENTRES OF EXPERTISE

Fig. 3.2 Bank of Scotland's structure
(Source: Bank of Scotland Report and Accounts 2000)

Organisation charts

AQA A AQA B
EDEXCEL
OCR A OCR B
WJEC
NICCEA

Organisations providing services in the public sector will be organised differently to those firms that have been set up to make profits for their owners.

The function of an organisation chart is to show the **internal structure** of a firm. The **departmental** structure of the firm in Fig. 3.1 can clearly be seen on the chart, which may be laid out **vertically** (as here) or **horizontally**. The chart shows the **status** of each manager and level, and the **communication lines** within the firm. We see that the Board of Directors and the Managing Director are at the top of the 'tree', and the different functions – each of which has its own internal structure – are then listed under the titles of the individual managers.

> **KEY POINT**
> An organisation chart illustrates the firm's hierarchy, the various levels of authority and responsibility that exist.

Organisational terms

AQA A AQA B
EDEXCEL
OCR A OCR B
WJEC
NICCEA

Fig. 3.1 shows the Works Manager's span of control is three (Production Controller, Chief Designer and Chief Inspector); the Marketing Manager's span is four; and so on.

We use a number of terms to describe the key features of an organisation.

Span of control

A person's 'span of control' is measured by **the number of staff directly controlled** by that person.

An important influence on a person's span of control is **the nature of the employee's work**: i.e., how much supervision is needed. Highly skilled work, for example, may require a lot of supervision, and so the supervisor's span of control will probably be limited to only a few employees. Too wide a span of control leads to inefficient supervision and control, and this may be reflected in the quality of the output.

Chain of command

The chain of command is shown clearly in the organisation chart (Fig. 3.1)

A firm's chain of command comes from its **hierarchical** structure. The chain highlights the different **status** of the various staff, running from the Board to the managers of the departments, then to the staff in these departments. It also shows who makes **decisions**, and who is **responsible** to whom.

'Tall' and 'flat' structures

An organisation's structure may be described as either 'tall' or 'flat'. This indicates the number of levels found in the organisation. Tall structures have long chains of command. This normally means:

● communication takes a long time to pass from top to bottom
● spans of control are usually narrow
● employees are usually specialised

> **KEY POINT**
> Many firms nowadays try to 'flatten' their organisational structure, to improve the speed of communication and to remove the 'them and us' feeling sometimes associated with tall structures.

Delegation, responsibility and authority

The Board and Managing Director can't take every decision needed. They **delegate** – pass down the chain of command – to their managers the responsibility of making day-to-day decisions. These managers will, in turn, delegate the more routine tasks to their own staff.

The normal source of people's authority to act comes from their job description (page 76).

Delegation of duties must be accompanied by giving the member of staff the **authority** to do these duties. The member of staff will then have the **responsibility** of doing the job.

If managers don't delegate properly, they may end up carrying out the more routine tasks that their staff should be doing: their time is not being used as efficiently as it should be. The other extreme is for the manager to delegate too much responsibility to staff, who then carry out tasks for which they shouldn't be responsible.

> **KEY POINT**
>
> The Board's role is to agree the long-term strategy for the firm, and to make strategic decisions to do with growth, new products, new markets and so on.

Centralisation and decentralisation

These terms can be linked to tall and flat structures, to the idea of authority, and to the amount of delegation taking place. For example, where there is a lot of delegation, decisions are being made at various levels in the firm, which is said to be **decentralised**. Where delegation is limited in the firm, this illustrates a **centralised** structure with the higher levels of management keeping control of the decision-making.

Line and staff organisation

The traditional organisation chart (Fig. 3.1) shows chains of command as a series of lines. This **line authority** exists in departments, though the **line managers** of these departments may be supported by specialists who aren't part of their department and who are not, therefore, in their line of command. These **staff** specialists advise line managers, and whole departments (such as Human Resources) may work on this basis.

In Fig. 3.1, the Company Secretary has a staff role.

PROGRESS CHECK

1. Identify **four** key functions for a large retail organisation.
2. State the difference between span of control and chain of command.

2. Span of control: the number of employees under the direct control of an individual. Chain of command: the line of formal communication in an organisation.

1. Marketing/selling; accounts; human resources; purchasing.

3.2 Communication in business

After studying this section you should be able to understand:

- **communication in trading**
- **internal and external communication**
- **visual communication**
- **storing and retrieving information**

Communication through trading

AQA A   AQA B
EDEXCEL
OCR   OCR
WJEC
NICCEA

We hear a lot about the 'paperless office', but in reality paper is still the most important medium of communication found in firms today.

The main trading documents

Firms involved in buying and selling have to record many transactions. The trading documents act as a **record** of events, and also as **proof** that a transaction has taken place.

A flow of documents takes place between the buyer and the seller, as illustrated in Fig. 3.3.

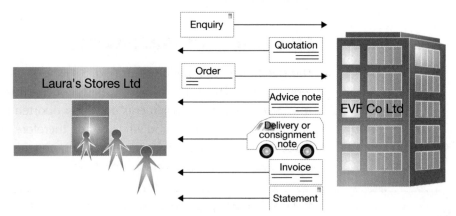

Fig. 3.3 Trading document flow

On receiving a **letter of enquiry**, the selling firm sends product details. If the buyer is interested, a **quotation** may be requested: this is sent, often with a catalogue and price list, by the seller. The **order** sent by the buyer indicates:

- the number of items ordered
- their description, catalogue number and price
- when and where they are to be delivered

The supplier may forward an **advice note** separately from the goods to tell the buyer they have been despatched. A **delivery note** is sent when the supplier delivers the goods (a **consignment note** may be sent if an independent carrier delivers them).

An **invoice** is shown on page 98. It contains details of the goods – their description, quantity, price and total cost – and the buyer may treat the invoice as a bill for payment. If the buyer is a regular customer, the seller will send at a later date a **statement of account**, which shows the buyer the goods sent and payments received in the period.

> Trade within the EU often uses the Single Administrative Document, which replaced many forms previously used to record the movement of goods in the EU.

KEY POINT

The invoice is the most important document used in trading: several copies are often produced (for the seller's accounts, sales and despatch departments), the top copy going to the buyer.

Internal and external communication

AQA A AQA B
EDEXCEL
OCR OCR
WJEC
NICCEA

There are several different and important stakeholder groups (page 44) in business: they include directors, shareholders, the local community, employees, customers and suppliers. The firm must communicate efficiently with members in all these groups. The process of communication used involves the:

- **sender**
- **message** being sent
- **medium** by which the message is sent
- **receiver** of the message

So, communication takes place both **internally** – within the firm – and **externally** – between the firm and another organisation or individual.

Internal written forms

> Letters are more associated with external communication, but are still an important form of internal communication.

Written communication is widely used to communicate both internally and externally.

- **Letters** are used internally on formal occasions, e.g. being sent to warn an employee whose behaviour could lead to dismissal, and to inform new staff of their contract.

  - **Memos** – the memorandum is the most widely used internal written form: less formal (e.g. it is not signed) and more concise than a letter, Fig. 3.4 illustrates a traditional written memo.
  - **Notices** and **company journals** are used in business to provide various written details, for example of company health and safety rules, or of its sports and social club activities. They are also used to publicise jobs internally.
  - Formal meetings within a firm are structured using a written **agenda**, and the results of the meeting are again written down, as **minutes** of the meeting.
  - Written **reports** are produced by individuals or committees. They tend to be formal documents on aspects such as the progress of a new product, or the expected effects of computerising an existing procedure.

Internal memorandum

G GABRIEL'S of WOLVERHAMPTON

From Sales Manager

To Sales Staff   date: 18 October

MOTOR INSURANCE

Following the opening of our Walsall branch, please ensure that your car motor insurance covers you for personal business use in addition to the normal social, domestic and pleasure cover.

Fig. 3.4 A memo

Memos in particular, but also all the other forms of written communication (normally as electronic attachments), are nowadays often sent using email.

We already know that trading documents are examples of external written communication, and that business letters are sent to customers, suppliers and other groups.

External written forms

The **annual report and accounts** of a limited company must be sent, by law, to all its shareholders. Page 113 explains what it contains, and the company will often present more 'user-friendly' information in terms of pictures, diagrams and summaries of the information.

Oral communication

The two main forms of oral communication are the telephone and meetings.

1. The **telephone** is used as both an internal and external method of communication. It has the advantage over business letters and memos that it is **faster and more flexible**, since it allows the caller to adapt the message, explaining any points that aren't understood. Nowadays email is, in practice, just as quick, and this written form of communication has the advantage over the telephone that it gives a more **permanent record** of the message.
2. **Meetings** may be informal, e.g. between a section head and a member of staff, or formal, being supported by an agenda and minutes.

KEY POINT   Perhaps the most important meeting is the AGM – annual general meeting – of a company, where directors are elected and the company's performance is discussed.

Visual communication

AQA A   AQA B
EDEXCEL
OCR A   OCR B
WJEC
NICCEA

The purpose of displaying information visually is to **simplify** and to **summarise** it. Visual communication is often used where **impact** is required to 'get the message across'. To communicate visually, firms choose from:

- charts and graphs
- pictures and photographs
- flowcharts and other technical diagrams
- maps and plans

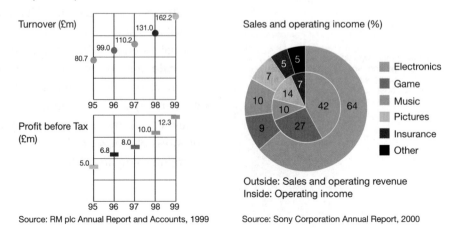

Fig. 3.5A Visual communication: ways to display financial information

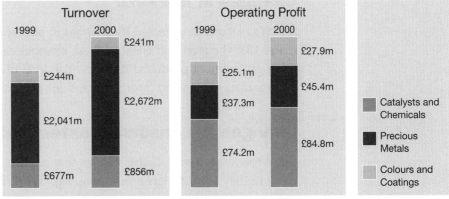

Source: Johnson Matthey Annual Report and Accounts, 2000

Fig. 3.5B Visual communication: ways to display financial information

Storing and retrieving information

AQA A   AQA B
EDEXCEL
OCR A   OCR B
WJEC
NICCEA

Records need to be kept and communicated by firms. These records include information on employees, products, stocks, and contracts, and there must be a system of record-keeping that allows the information to be **stored**, **retrieved** and **transmitted** (sent).

An efficient record-keeping system must have these qualities.

1. It must be capable of being **expanded** when necessary.
2. It must be **easily understood** by its users.
3. The information must be **easily accessible**.
4. It must be **secure** from those who aren't entitled to use it.
5. The information must be **safe from deterioration**.

PROGRESS CHECK

1. Name the main features of communication.
2. State **three** features of a good communication system.

2. Capable of expansion; easily accessible; safe from deterioration.

1. Sender; message; medium; receiver.

3.3 The impact of change

LEARNING SUMMARY

After studying this section you should be able to understand:

● *the major changes taking place in our economy*
● *why people resist change*

Changes taking place

AQA A   AQA B
EDEXCEL
OCR A   OCR B
WJEC
NICCEA

The UK's economy is **dynamic**, i.e. it is ever-changing. Managers of some firms wait for changes to take place, and then react to these changes. Other managers may have a more positive approach, seeking to influence the way that change takes place.

Changes in markets

A firm's markets are affected by changes in **population** size and structure (page 18). The level and effect of these changes can be predicted by firms, using government-produced statistics. The level of **prices** and **incomes** are other factors influencing future demand for products.

Changes in consumer tastes and social attitudes

Consumer **tastes and fashions** also change, but these are harder to forecast because they're much less predictable. Fig. 3.6 illustrates how spending patterns can change.

Percentage of spending by families, 1970 and 2000

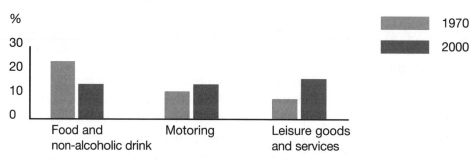

Fig. 3.6 Changes in family spending over the last 30 years (Source: ONS)

> Many multinationals, which sell tobacco products in developing economies, have diversified because the trend in advanced economies has been to stop smoking.

Changes in **social attitudes** are difficult to predict. Some firms may try to counter the changes in demand for their products by **diversifying** into different products and markets.

Changes in technology

In production, **CAD/CAM** (see page 151) and other computer-based developments are commonly found in today's manufacturing firms. **Automatic handling** systems for materials are also widely used. We also know that **increased consumer access** to computers and the Internet has brought about the development of **e-commerce** (page 141).

Fig. 3.7 The 'new technology' influences the economy

Resisting change

AQA A   AQA B
EDEXCEL
OCR A   OCR B
WJEC
NICCEA

There are many 'computer skills' courses available for adults who wish to return to the job market.

The effects of change on employees include encouraging (or making) them **develop new skills** to cope with new working practices. There is **greater job mobility** because the pace of technological change is leading to the decline of old jobs and industries, with new ones springing up to replace them. One feature is an **increase in leisure time** and interest in leisure activities, as shown by Fig. 3.6.

Employees may **resist** change for these reasons.

- **Loss of power or status**. Changes which lead to a person losing power or status may be resisted.
- **Fear and insecurity**. Many employees become concerned that they won't be able to cope with the changes being introduced at work.
- **Personal reasons**. Changes resulting in a person being put under pressure, e.g. by having to move job and/or area, may be resisted.

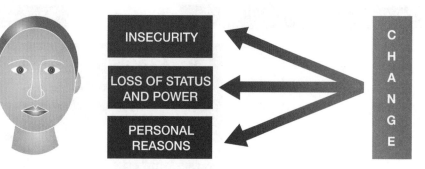

Fig. 3.8 Resisting change

PROGRESS CHECK

1. In what ways does change occur in today's economy?

1. Changes in markets; in taste and social attitudes; in technology.

3.4 Size and growth

LEARNING SUMMARY

After studying this section you should be able to understand:
- *how we measure the size of a business*
- *how firms grow*

How we measure 'size'

AQA A   AQA B
EDEXCEL
OCR A   OCR B
WJEC
NICCEA

We find that businesses grow in size for a number of reasons.

- Larger size leads to **economies of scale** (see page 148), which make a firm more competitive.
- A larger firm usually has a **better chance of surviving** in the business world: it will gain a greater market share, it can borrow funds more easily, and it will probably rely less on the profitability of a single product.

● The owners and/or the directors may seek the **power and status** that come from being in charge of a larger firm, so they may try to expand its operations.

How do we measure size? The most popular criteria – 'measuring tools' – used are **turnover**, **net profit**, **capital employed** and the **number of employees**. Fig. 3.9 illustrates how two of our best-known retailers, Sainsbury's and Tesco, measured up recently. It shows that Tesco is the larger if we use turnover and profits to measure size, but Sainsbury's has more employees and more capital employed.

	Profits before tax £ million	Turnover £ million
Tesco	842	17,158
Sainsbury	832	15,196

	Capital employed £ million	Employees
Sainsbury	4,663	177,906
Tesco	4,377	172,712

Fig. 3.9 Comparing size
(Source: annual accounts of J Sainsbury plc and Tesco plc, 1999)

> We should compare firms in the same industry using the same measure of size.

● **Turnover** (net sales, i.e. sales less VAT) is the most popular way to compare the size of firms.
● A firm's **net profit** figure can be a good indicator of its size, although different firms in the same industry operate using different profit margins.
● The '**capital employed**' figure shows the net investment in a firm, but this can prove to be a difficult figure to measure.
● The **number of employees** will be influenced by a firm's size: many firms (such as Sainsbury's and Tesco) have both full-time and part-time staff, which may make this a difficult measure to use.

Internal expansion

The size of a business will vary from year to year. Many firms grow **organically**, naturally through **internal expansion**, by:

1. producing and selling more of its products in its existing markets
2. selling these products in new markets or market segments
3. making and selling new products

> **KEY POINT** The firm normally finances internal growth by keeping and using some of its profits: these retained profits are being 'ploughed back'.

How firms grow

AQA A AQA B
EDEXCEL
OCR A OCR B
WJEC
NICCEA

As well as growing naturally, many companies also try to grow more quickly by deciding to take over, or merge with, existing businesses. **Integration** is the name we give to **external growth**.

A company's shares being traded on the stock exchange brings the risk of being taken over.

- A **takeover** occurs when one company buys enough of another company's voting shares in order to allow it to take control. The directors of the company being taken over may try to oppose it but may be powerless to stop it.
- A **merger** takes place between two companies through their agreement (unlike many takeovers). The two companies are usually completely reorganised following the merger.

EMI takes £43m hit for failed merger

Big move in shares amid merger talk

SmithKline and Glaxo near merger go-ahead

Abbey and BoS admit to top level merger talks

Companies merging

Shire in £5.9bn merger

Merger mania – coming to a company near you

Fig. 3.10 Mergers in the news

Integration by either merger or take over allows the new company to expand quickly. There are three forms of integration:

1. **horizontal** integration
2. **vertical** integration
3. **lateral** (or **conglomerate**) integration

Fig. 3.11 summarises these three forms.

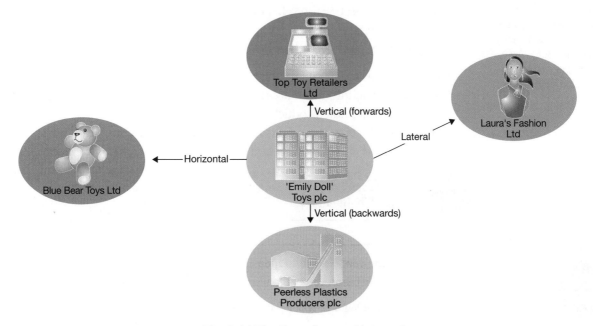

Fig. 3.11 The three forms of integration

Horizontal integration

A horizontal merger or takeover occurs between firms **in the same industry** and **at the same stage of production**. We find many recent examples in the financial sector of our economy, including the insurance companies Norwich Union and Commercial & General, and the banks Lloyds and TSB.

> **KEY POINT**
>
> **Horizontal integration leads to** large-scale production **and economies of scale, and a** larger market share **giving greater market power.**

Vertical integration

This form of integration also takes place between firms in the same industry, but which are at **different stages of production**. Many breweries control their own public houses, tyre manufacturers own rubber plantations, and oil companies have their own refineries and filling stations.

Vertical backwards integration occurs when the company starts to control the firms that supply its raw materials: it is moving back down the chain of production. This form of integration means that:

1. the company is now directly in control of the **supply**, **quality** and **delivery** of its raw materials
2. the **profits** of the firm under its control now belong to the company
3. **economies of scale** are likely

Vertical forwards integration is found where a company merges with, or takes over, firms further along the chain of production (e.g. a producer taking over a retail outlet). The advantages for the controlling company here also include owning the profits of the firm under its control, and gaining from economies of scale. In addition, it has **better access to its market**, e.g. by being able to control advertising and promotion.

Lateral integration

British–American Tobacco plc, for example, has taken over companies such as Yardley (cosmetics), Argos (retailing) and Eagle Star (insurance).

We also know this as 'conglomerate' or 'diversified' integration: it occurs where **firms in different industries** integrate. One example of conglomerate integration is where tobacco companies, faced with falling UK demand for their main products, take over other firms in expanding areas of our economy.

The advantages of lateral integration are:
1. by diversifying into other areas, **risk is reduced** – the company no longer depends on a single product
2. a company's current products may dominate, or 'saturate', the market – it can't expand in this market, and so it seeks **new markets** for its expansion

> **KEY POINT**
>
> **The results of growth are** economies of scale: we study these in detail in Chapter 8.

> **PROGRESS CHECK**
>
> 1. List the **four** ways we use to measure the size of a business.
> 2. Distinguish between vertical forwards and vertical backwards integration.
>
> 1. Turnover; profits; capital employed; employees.
> 2. Forwards: integration towards the consumer. Backwards: integration towards the point of supply.

Sample GCSE questions

This question is about the effect of a possible takeover.

British Rod Mills Ltd. (known as BRM) produce steel rods which are used mainly in the building industry to produce reinforced concrete. The material used to make the rods is scrap metal from old cars and cookers. The scrap is melted down at their own steel works where large blocks of steel are produced.

Some of the steel produced is sold to other businesses but most is used to produce rods which are either sold to the building industry or are further processed to make wire and then nails.

SCRAP ⟶ STEEL ⟶ RODS ⟶ WIRE ⟶ NAILS

The Board of Directors at BRM is considering taking over a scrap metal yard and a competing rod producer, called MegaRod.

(a) Which types of integration are involved if BRM takes over both (i) a scrap metal yard and (ii) a competing producer? **(2)**

　(i) This is 'vertical backwards' integration.
　(ii) This is horizontal integration.

Accurate answers.

(b) Explain the benefits that BRM could face from owning businesses at each stage of production from scrap to nails. **(6)**

If BRM take over the scrap yard it will have control of its supply, so it is more in control of events. BRM will receive the profits that previously went to the scrap yard. If BRM takes over the competitor, it will again have the company's profits. It will have less competition in the marketplace and a bigger market share.

This is the main point to make, but you need to explain 'more in control of events': make more precise points, e.g. 'BRM is now in control of the quality and the delivery of its materials'.

Also explain the production-based benefits, e.g. that there will be greater economies of scale.

(c) Explain the likely effects on the workforces at **both** BRM and MegaRod if the proposed takeover goes ahead. **(6)**

I expect some of the workforce at both places will be surplus to requirements. MegaRod's workforce is probably worse off, because they may use different methods of production. Some of BRM's staff may also not be needed now.

Correct, but what is the relevance to the workforce? You need to explain the effects: these could include redundancy and the offer of early retirement. A good point is made about MegaRod's staff being more affected, but relate it to the needs of the remaining workforce: e.g. they will have to be trained to follow BRM's approach.

WJEC Paper 2, 2000

Exam practice questions

This is a question on the structure of an organisation.

1.

```
                         ┌─────────────────────┐
                         │  Managing Director  │
                         └─────────────────────┘
```

| Human Resources Director (Head of Personnel Department) | Sales Director (Head of Sales Department) | Finance Director (Head of Finance Department) |

| Recruitment Manager | Staff Welfare Manager | North Region Manager | South Region Manager | Customer Accounts Manager | Expenditure Manager |

| 8 Office Staff | 5 Office Staff | 15 Sales People | 15 Sales People | 10 Office Staff | 8 Office Staff |

(a) Name **one** department, other than Personnel, Sales or Accounts,
which the firm might have but which has been left out of this chart. **(1)**

....

(b) **(i)** What is meant by the term *span of control*? **(2)**

....

(ii) What is the span of control of the Recruitment Manager? **(1)**

....

(iii) Which person on this chart is responsible for the whole business? **(1)**

....

(iv) Who does the Customer Accounts Manager first report
to if there is a serious problem? **(1)**

....

(c) Suggest and explain **two** reasons why businesses use organisational structures
like the one above. **(4)**

....

....

(d) Describe the work done by (i) the Sales Department and (ii) the Accounts Department in
this business. **(6)**

....

....

....

WJEC Paper 1, 2000

The following topics are included in this chapter:

- **The European Union**
- **Controlling business activity**
- **Supporting business activity**

4.1 The European Union

LEARNING SUMMARY

After studying this section you should be able to understand:

- **the influence of the EU**
- **the single currency**

The EU's influence

`AQA A` `AQA B`
`EDEXCEL`
`OCR A` `OCR B`
`WJEC`
`NICCEA`

> The number of countries in the EU is expected to increase dramatically in the first decade of the twenty-first century.

The European Union (EU) was established in 1957 by the **Treaty of Rome**. It now consists of 15 members.

Original members, 1957		1972	1980	1986	1995
Belgium	Luxembourg	UK	Greece	Portugal	Austria
France	Netherlands	Denmark		Spain	Finland
Italy	(West) Germany	Ireland		Sweden	

Fig. 4.1 EU membership

The EU and trade

> The EU's Single Administrative Document was introduced in 1988, and has simplified the paperwork that supports trade in the EU.

- **Subsidies** are provided, e.g. to those working in agriculture through the **Common Agricultural Policy** (CAP). This helps control food prices for EU consumers and supports employment in this sector, although the CAP has been criticised for creating 'butter mountains', 'wine lakes' and other surpluses.
- **Free movement of capital and labour** exists in the EU's **Single Market**, taking place between member states and helping to increase trade.
- The Single Market also means that there are **no internal trade barriers**: the EU's **Common External Tariff** (CET) means that goods coming into the EU – wherever they enter – are subject to the same tariff.
- **Open markets** in areas such as IT and telecommunications have led to

common standards being set, and equipment made by British companies must meet these standards.

- The Single Market in areas such as **financial services** and **transport** have led to British firms being able to (and having to) compete with other EU companies in these areas.

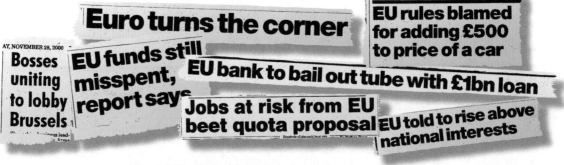

Euro turns the corner

EU rules blamed for adding £500 to price of a car

AY, NOVEMBER 28, 2000

Bosses uniting to lobby Brussels

EU funds still misspent, report says

EU bank to bail out tube with £1bn loan

Jobs at risk from EU beet quota proposal

EU told to rise above national interests

Fig. 4.2 The EU influences our economy

> **KEY POINT**
> Establishing the Common External Tariff has encouraged many overseas multinationals to produce their goods inside the EU, to avoid the CET.

Fig. 4.3 shows just how important the EU is as a trading area for the UK.

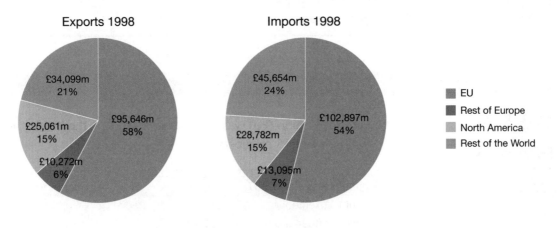

Exports 1998

£34,099m 21%
£25,061m 15%
£10,272m 6%
£95,646m 58%

Imports 1998

£45,654m 24%
£28,782m 15%
£13,095m 7%
£102,897m 54%

- EU
- Rest of Europe
- North America
- Rest of the World

Fig. 4.3 The EU: our main trading partner

The euro debate

AQA A AQA B
EDEXCEL
OCR A OCR B
WJEC
NICCEA

The **euro** is the **single currency** that was adopted by 11 of the EU member states from 1999 (Greece has also now joined). Although the UK didn't join on that date, our firms are still affected, especially those trading in the 'euro zone'.

Because the UK didn't adopt the single currency in 1999, the euro is foreign currency and won't be legal tender here unless we join in the future.

Fig. 4.4 The euro

What the single currency means

- The euro makes **price differences** more obvious throughout the euro zone.
- It gets rid of the need to **change currencies**, and therefore avoids **exchange rate fluctuations** for exporters and importers.

The practical issues for UK firms include having to **handle and record** the euro (e.g. in their accounts), consider how they **price their products** if they trade in the euro zone, and **change their systems**, such as IT and stock control, to recognise the euro.

> **KEY POINT**
>
> **UK firms most affected by the euro will be** importers **and** exporters **trading in the euro zone,** multinational firms **operating in Europe, and** banks **and other organisations working in European financial markets.**

PROGRESS CHECK

1. State how membership of the EU affects UK traders.

1. There are open markets, with no trade barriers and free movement of capital and labour.

4.2 Controlling business activity

LEARNING SUMMARY

After studying this section you should be able to understand:

- *the ways that firms are influenced*
- *protecting competition, consumers and employees*
- *pressure groups*

Influences on business

All businesses – whether they are run to make profits for their owners, or to provide a service for the public – will be influenced by their environment. The activities of firms, just like those of people, are affected by a wide range of laws, regulations and other organisations. Some of these will **support** business activity: others will **control** it.

Any organisation faces control of many of its activities, for example its:

- **location** and **development**, e.g. planning permission laws, and government regional policy (page 22)
- **relationship with its employees**, e.g. protecting staff through health and safety laws
- **relationship with its consumers**, e.g. weights and measures regulations
- **taxation and financial policies**, e.g. having to pay VAT and corporation tax (on its profits) to the government

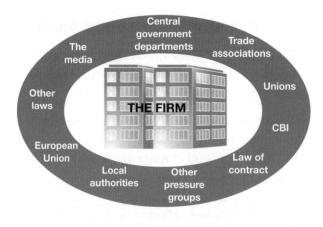

Fig. 4.5 Influences on firms

Protecting competition

AQA A AQA B
EDEXCEL
OCR A OCR B
WJEC
NICCEA

Competition law

The **Fair Trading Act** of 1973 set up the **Office of Fair Trading** (OFT), under the control of a Director-General of Fair Trading. Trading matters are examined, and any '**restrictive practices**' are controlled. The **Competition Act** of 1980 deals with anti-competitive practices.

> The Competition Commission replaced the Monopolies and Mergers Commission in 1998.

The **Competition Commission** works closely with the OFT. It checks whether any proposed merger between two large companies would lead to a situation that is not in the interest of consumers.

The EU operates a '**Competition Policy**', which also seeks to control the number and level of monopolies in its member countries. Its **Merger Control Regulation** is designed to ensure that trade in the EU takes place on a free and fair basis.

> **KEY POINT**
>
> Monopolies are discouraged in the private sector: here, firms operate through the profit margin, and competition should provide consumers with low prices and a variety of goods.

Protecting consumers

AQA A AQA B
EDEXCEL
OCR A OCR B
WJEC
NICCEA

The law of contract

This forms the legal basis of the transactions that take place between firms, between a firm and its employees (the contract of employment), and between a firm and its consumers. A contract is a **legal agreement** between people: a limited company is a 'person' in the eyes of the law. Most contracts are entered into by firms very easily, such as over the telephone. Other contracts – for example, to do with buying and selling property – are more formal.

> If a business can't meet its obligations under a typical trading contract, it will probably have to pay damages – financial compensation – to the other party in the contract.

Government control

The government has set up various 'watchdogs' that **regulate** the former nationalised industries. Examples include **OFTEL**, the telecommunications regulator, and **OFWAT**, which oversees the water industry.

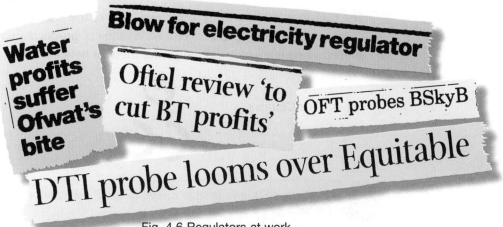

Fig. 4.6 Regulators at work

Local authorities also provide consumer protection: they employ people in trading standards and environmental health, and offer advice on consumer-related issues.

UK consumer protection laws

There are many UK Acts and EU Directives that firms must obey when selling goods or providing services.

UK laws relating to the sale of goods and services include the following.

- The **Sale and Supply of Goods Act** 1994 brought together various other Acts relating to the sale of goods. Under this Act, goods must be of **satisfactory quality**, i.e. they must be fit to be sold. They must also be **fit for the purpose for which they were bought** and, if sold by description, they must **match their description**.
- The **Supply of Goods and Services Act** 1982 extended the protection given under Sale of Goods law to services such as package holidays and hairdressing.
- The **Unsolicited Goods and Services Act** 1971 stops firms delivering, and then demanding payment for, items sent to people who have not ordered them.
- The **Trade Descriptions Acts** (1968 and 1972) make it a criminal offence to give a false description of goods or services.

Consumers are also protected by the **Food Safety Act** (1990), which controls the supply of food products, and by the **Consumer Credit Act** 1974 and the **Financial Services Act** 1986, which control people or businesses offering financial services, e.g. by making them become registered.

The Disability Discrimination Act (1995) makes it unlawful for those providing goods, services and facilities to discriminate against disabled people.

EU Directives on consumer protection

Examples of EU Directives on consumer protection include the following.

- **Electronic Commerce** – this Directive makes information providers give certain information (e.g. name and address, prices) to people using e-commerce.
- **Misleading Advertising** – this Directive protects people against unfair advertising practices.
- **Doorstep Selling** – this provides a one-week 'cooling off' period if certain goods are bought at home.
- **Toy Safety** – this Directive harmonises (standardises) toy safety standards.
- **Price Indication** – this harmonises the display of selling prices in member states.

The EU issues '**CE Marking**' Directives. One of the first concerned the safety of children's toys, and others cover a wide range of products such as personal protective equipment, machinery, and medical devices.

Fig. 4.7 The CE mark

> **KEY POINT**
>
> **UK and EU laws provide a wide range of consumer protection, for both goods and services.**

Protecting employees

AQA A AQA B
EDEXCEL
OCR A OCR B
WJEC
NICCEA

Employment and dismissal

We know that a firm's permanent staff are employed under a **contract of employment**, which must contain certain information (page 79). Workers are protected against **unfair dismissal**: an employee who wants to pursue a claim of unfair dismissal can, with union help, involve ACAS (page 93) in the dispute. If this fails, an **industrial tribunal** will decide if the dismissal was unfair. If a case of unfair dismissal is found, the employee will be entitled to compensation, reinstatement to the original job, or re-engagement in a new job.

The **Data Protection Act** 1998 requires employers to follow certain procedures with manual and computer-based **records**, including recruitment and employment records. It has helped bring about a code of practice about **employee monitoring**: in particular, whether the employer can check if staff use emails and access to the Internet for personal reasons.

> 'There is no Data Protection provision that requires an employer to allow employees to use the employer's telephone system, email system or Internet access for personal communications ...'

Fig. 4.8 Controlling employees who have access to emails and the Internet
(Source: the Data Protection Commissioner, 2000)

In the UK, we have a longer working week than most other EU countries.

The national minimum wage also came about through EU membership.

There have been many recent changes to UK employment law as a result of our membership of the EU. For example:

- the **Working Time Regulations**, which limit working hours to a normal maximum of 48
- the **Parental Leave Directive**, giving staff a right to unpaid leave following the birth of a child
- the **Part-time Work Directive**, which ensures equal treatment for part-time staff

Discrimination

The **Equal Pay Act** 1970 forces employers to pay men and women who are doing similar work equal rates of pay for this work. This Act, which was reinforced by an EU Directive in 1975, is one form of protection against sexual discrimination. Further protection comes from the **Sex Discrimination Acts** (1975 and 1987). The conditions of these Acts make it unlawful for an employer to discriminate on the grounds of sex when advertising a job, employing a person or setting a retirement date. People who believe they have been discriminated against can approach the **Equal Opportunities Commission** (EOC) for advice.

According to the EOC, in 1999 the UK was ranked only tenth out of the 15 EU countries for the equality of its pay.

Industrial tribunals may again consider cases of sexual or racial discrimination.

The **Race Relations Acts** (1968 and 1976) make it illegal for an employer to discriminate against a person on the grounds of race, nationality or ethnic origin. If a person suspects discrimination has taken place in areas such as recruitment, promotion or dismissal, he or she can approach the **Commission for Racial Equality** for help.

The **Disability Discrimination Act** (1995) makes it unlawful to discriminate against employing a person on the grounds of his or her disability.

> **KEY POINT**
> Employers are more and more aware of how important it is to operate non-discrimination policies.

Health and safety

In 1974 the **Health and Safety at Work Act** (HASAWA) was passed. It states the duties of the employer and the employee regarding health and safety at work.

The employer's duties	The employee's duties
to provide safe: • **working conditions** • **machinery** • **working processes** • **entry and exit arrangements**	• to take **reasonable care of themselves and others** whilst at work • **not to interfere with** anything provided for their own safety or the safety of others • to **report any defects** in equipment, work areas etc. • to **co-operate with the employer** over health and safety matters

The **Health and Safety Executive** (HSE) helps enforce the law, as well as providing information and advice, and carrying out research into health and safety matters.

Pressure groups and other organisations

AQA A   AQA B
EDEXCEL
OCR A   OCR B
WJEC
NICCEA

We have many influential pressure groups in the UK. A pressure group is an organised group of people with similar interests, who attempt to influence others. They may work locally, such as when **local residents' associations** try to influence their local council or local business. Many '**cause**' pressure groups are national or international, having grown in importance as a result of concern about human rights, health and environmental matters. Groups such as **Amnesty International, Friends of the Earth, Greenpeace** and **ASH** (Action on Smoking and Health) influence firms through action such as campaigning for new laws.

Pressure groups in the business world include the TUC and trade unions (page 89), the CBI (page 92), and chambers of commerce (page 92).

Here are examples of influential national pressure groups or other organisations that protect either particular consumer groups or consumers as a whole.

- The **Advertising Standards Authority** (ASA) protects consumers by controlling the advertising standards of firms through its code of advertising practice (TV advertising is controlled by the Independent Television Commission).
- The **AA** and the **RAC** are motoring organisations that campaign on behalf of the motorist.
- The **Association of British Travel Agents** (ABTA) helps safeguard the holidays of customers who book with one of its member firms, and keeps a central fund to provide compensation.
- The **Consumers' Association** tests goods and services, and then reports on them to its members in its '**Which?**' series of magazines.
- The **UK media** often carry out investigations on behalf of the public. Newspapers, TV (with programmes such as 'Watchdog') and radio publicise the activities of firms and individuals who may be carrying out unfair or inefficient business practices.

Fig. 4.9 ABTA and the RAC: two organisations that protect consumer groups

PROGRESS CHECK

1. In what ways are consumers protected?
2. What is a 'pressure group'?

2. An organised group of people with similar interests, who attempt to influence others.

1. By UK laws, e.g. on sale of goods and supply of services; regulators such as OFTEL; EU Directives, e.g. on advertising, selling, prices and safety.

4.3 Supporting business activity

LEARNING SUMMARY

After studying this section you should be able to understand:
- *the range of support available*
- *how government and other agencies support business*

The range of support

AQA A   AQA B
EDEXCEL
OCR A   OCR B
WJEC
NICCEA

Many of the organisations that control business activity also help to support it. This help may come from local or central government, the European Union, or non-government sources such as trade associations and chambers of commerce.

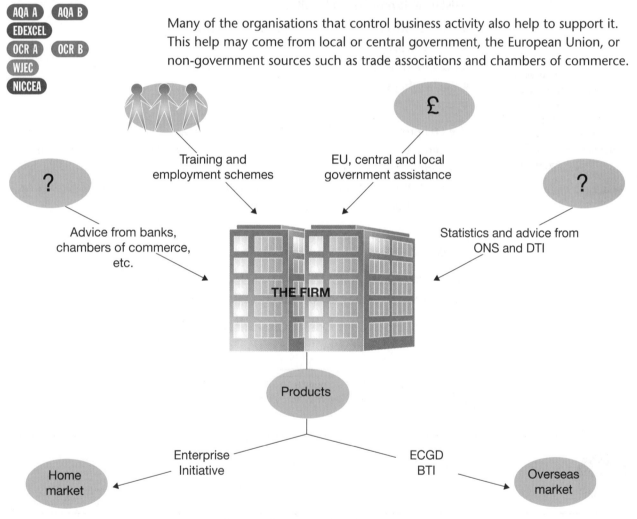

Fig. 4.10 Sources of aid for business

Government and other aid

AQA A   AQA B
EDEXCEL
OCR A   OCR B
WJEC
NICCEA

Financial support

The government provides a range of financial support, especially to new firms and to the regions (page 22). The EU also provides financial support, e.g. through its **Regional Development Fund** and **Social Fund** (e.g. for training)

The ONS, with offices in Newport (South Wales), Southport and Fareham, is a good example of how the government distributes some of its work throughout the country.

Information

The UK government provides a range of publications and information services, which are designed to help firms trading in both home and overseas markets. The **Office for National Statistics** (ONS) is the government's main provider of general statistical information. Its publications include the 'Annual Abstract of Statistics', 'Social Trends' (details of population, employment, income and wealth), and 'Regional Trends' (information on regional and national changes).

Banks, local **chambers of commerce** and **trade associations** are other examples of important sources of information for firms.

The Department of Trade and Industry (DTI)

The DTI plays an important role in providing UK business with advice and assistance. It provides help with:

- **European matters**, e.g. on product standards
- **regulations**
- how to improve **business performance** and how to **expand**,
- **technology**
- **environmental matters**

Help with environmental matters includes the DTI Recycling Programme, which seeks to boost demand for recycled materials.

The DTI provides a lot of advice for **small businesses** and **new businesses**, including its **Small Business Service** of information about support schemes and various regulations, and its network of **Business Links** (England), **Business Shops** (Scotland), **Business Connect** offices (Wales) and **EDnet** (Northern Ireland), all of which act as local business advice centres.

Exporting

British Trade International (BTI) helps UK firms take advantage of overseas business opportunities, by providing advice and assistance with exporting.

The role of the **Export Credit Guarantee Department** (ECGD) is to support exporters by giving guarantees and providing insurance for UK exports.

> **KEY POINT**
>
> The government wants to encourage economic growth, **for example** to help provide full employment.

PROGRESS CHECK

1. In what ways does the UK government support business?
2. Name **four** other sources of support available to UK firms.

2. Banks; chambers of commerce; trade associations; the EU.
1. Providing information; providing finance; supporting exports.

Sample GCSE questions

This question is about Britain's membership of the EU.

1. Since the start of the *Single Market* in 1991, the European Union has in effect become the domestic market of many British firms.

(a) What do you understand by the term *Single Market*? (2)

> `Single Market´ means we have a single country, economically speaking, in the European Union.

You need to explain that membership of the Single Market means that there are no restrictions on trade between the members of the EU.

(b) Assess the **advantages** and **disadvantages** which membership of the European Union has created for British firms. (8)

> Membership of the EU brings many advantages to Britain. These include being able to trade at an advantage with other EU members, because we don't have to pay the Common External Tariff that non-EU members have to pay. There is free movement of labour and capital, so this helps British people find jobs elsewhere but also means that some British jobs may go to members of other EU countries. One of the problems for British firms is the competition that membership of the EU's Single Market brings.

WJEC Specimen Paper 2

This is correct, but remember that this may lead to problems with our non-EU trading partners.

British firms gain from being able to recruit highly skilled staff from the rest of the EU.

A good point, but also mention that British firms can compete in the rest of the EU. It is also important to consider the issues to do with the Single Currency (e.g. adopting the euro would avoid currency fluctuation problems).

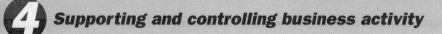

Exam practice questions

This is a question on how firms are supported, and how their employees may react to change.

1. Merchant Electronics Ltd. is a large manufacturing firm producing components for TV sets. It has recently introduced new technology to help produce these components, so that it can meet a new order from overseas. This is its first order from abroad.

    (a) What benefits will the new technology bring to Merchant Electronics' production? **(2)**

    ....

    ....

    (b) Describe **two** sources of information available to Merchant Electronics which will help it in its new role as an exporter. **(4)**

    ....

    ....

    ....

    ....

    (c) What attitude might the trade union adopt to the introduction of the new technology? **(4)**

    ....

    ....

    ....

    ....

5 Managing human resources

The following topics are included in this chapter:

- People and work
- Employing people
- Training people

- Motivation and job satisfaction
- Paying people
- Labour relations

5.1 People and work

LEARNING SUMMARY

After studying this section you should be able to understand:

- the role of the Human Resources function
- the work of a Human Resources department

The Human Resources function

AQA A AQA B
EDEXCEL
OCR A OCR B
WJEC
NICCEA

The role of the 'Human Resources function' is to deal with people who work, and those wish to work, in a firm. The larger organisations have a specialist Human Resources Department. We've summarised the range of work carried out by Human Resources in Fig. 5.1.

The Human Resources Department may also be known by its other name: the Personnel Department.

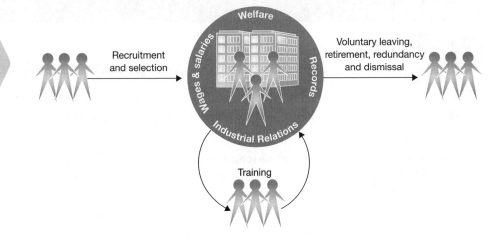

Fig. 5.1 The work of Human Resources

As the firm expands or as its employees retire or leave for other jobs, new staff have to be recruited. The role of Human Resources (HR) in **recruitment** is to inform potential employees that there are vacancies available. Following the advertising of these vacancies, HR Department staff work with their colleagues from the departments with the vacancies to **select** the best applicant for the job.

The new staff will be given **training**. All employees benefit from training, so the HR Department also provides training opportunities for existing staff. Human Resources work is also concerned with **staff welfare**. High levels of motivation lead to a happy and contented workforce, which in turn leads to high-quality output being produced. HR staff are involved in ensuring that minimum health, safety and other standards are met, and they may also be asked for help by employees facing work-related or personal problems. If necessary, HR department staff will be involved in **disciplining** or **dismissing** employees.

Details of staff are kept by Human Resources, as **staff records**. These details include personal information such as home address, as well as work-related information on pay, training courses attended and promotions received. Since Human Resources deals with employee records, it may also be responsible for calculating and distributing the **wages and salaries**, and for negotiating and developing the firm's pay structure. One of its key roles linked to this negotiation is **labour relations**: the HR Department has an important part to play in helping resolve disputes (and in avoiding them in the first place).

5.2 Employing people

After studying this section you should be able to understand:

- **recruiting staff**
- **how staff are selected**
- **appointing staff**

Recruitment

AQA A   AQA B
EDEXCEL
OCR A   OCR B
WJEC
NICCEA

Job description and person specification

The department with the vacancy will consider both the **type of work** the post requires, and the **type of person** best suited to this work.

> The information in the job description and person specification are used for the job advert.

The job description	The person specification
Details of the **work**:	Details of the **person**:
● job title and location	● personal qualities
● details of the duties	● expected qualifications
● any special features of the job	● work experience
● any special equipment used	● physical/mental abilities required

Job advertisements

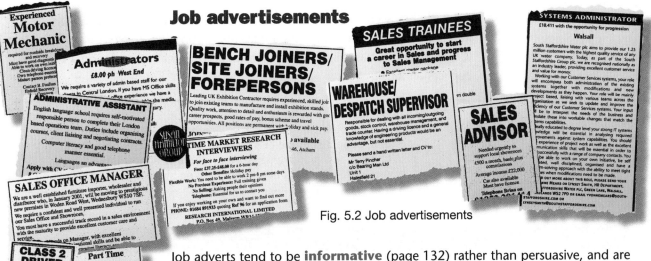

Fig. 5.2 Job advertisements

Job adverts tend to be **informative** (page 132) rather than persuasive, and are subject to laws which make sure that they don't discriminate in a racist or sexist manner (these legal controls are described in Chapter 4).

The firm may advertise **internally**. Adverts are displayed on noticeboards, sent to staff using a company circular, or published in its magazine. Filling the post from existing staff can be **quicker and less expensive** than from outside: it also **improves morale** because staff realise that promotion is possible. With internal appointments, however, **no 'new blood' is introduced**, which could lead to fewer new ideas.

If the post is to be advertised **externally**, Human Resources staff must decide where to advertise. Popular places for the advert to be displayed are listed below.

> Email is an increasingly popular way of circulating staff vacancies.

JOBCENTRE

Job : Toolsetter   (MAN OR WOMAN)
Distrtct : Halesfield
Wage : Up to £14.2
Hours : 2–10, 10–6, 6–2
Details : EXP. PERSON REQUIRED FOR SECOND OPERATION WORK TO INCLUDE DRILLING, MILLING & SPECIAL PURPOSE MULTI-HEAD MACHINES

ES 102 (JC)

Fig. 5.3 JobCentre advertisement

- **JobCentres**. Run by the Department for Education and Employment, these are located throughout the country, advertising vacancies supplied to them by local companies.
- **Employment agencies**. A firm may send details of a job vacancy to a local or national agency such as Pertemps or Brook Street Bureau. These agencies then check their records for people who have registered with them, and provide potential staff for interview. They receive a fee if the person is appointed, or (often in the case of temporary staff) the firm pays the agency, which in turn pays the person.

- **Newspapers and magazines**. Many professional and managerial vacancies are advertised in the 'quality' newspapers, or in specialist magazines or journals of the professional bodies. Local papers are also used for managerial, clerical and manual vacancies.

Application forms

Interested applicants normally have to complete a **job application form**, in which they give details of their education and experience. They are also asked to provide **references** from people who are prepared to support their application.

As an alternative to sending out a standard application form, the Human Resources Department might ask applicants to submit a **curriculum vitae**: this 'CV' will contain basically the same information as that asked for on a typical application form.

> **KEY POINT**
>
> All firms need to recruit:
> - to **replace** staff who have left for another job, or those who have retired, been dismissed or promoted to new posts within the firm
> - to bring in **new skills** required (e.g. where IT specialists are employed to bring in a new computerised system)

Selection

AQA A   AQA B
EDEXCEL
OCR A   OCR B
WJEC
NICCEA

Once applications are received, decisions must be made about which applicants to **short list**. The short list is drawn up by eliminating those applicants who don't meet the person specification: for example, they may be regarded as too inexperienced or overqualified. Laws relating to racial and sexual discrimination, and discrimination against people who have a disability, must be observed.

The interview

At an interview the **interviewer** can:

1. check whether the interviewee's **communication skills** are up to the required standard
2. assess the interviewee's **social skills**
3. Check their **physical appearance** (regarded as important for some jobs, e.g. sales force, receptionist)
4. see how **confident** the interviewee is
5. discuss information on the **application form**
6. judge whether the interviewee will **work effectively** with colleagues in the department

The **interviewee** can:

We often forget that an interview is a two-way process.

1. discuss **future prospects**, such as the possibility of promotion
2. check the **working conditions**
3. ask about **training** and other opportunities
4. judge the friendliness or otherwise of the **existing staff**
5. see the **facilities** available

Selection tests

Some firms run a series of tests to help decide which of the short-listed applicants is most suitable for the post. These tests may be designed to assess a candidate's intelligence, personality or aptitude (suitability) for the post.

- **Intelligence tests** are designed to check an applicant's mental abilities, and may involve testing verbal and numerical reasoning.
- **Personality tests** try to discover an applicant's personality, attitudes and beliefs in an attempt to find out whether he or she will fit happily into the company.

The diagrams on the left of the page follow a logical sequence. You are to select the next diagram in the series from the options on the right.

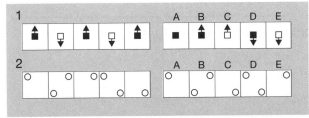

- **Aptitude tests** are set if the employer wants to see the applicant carrying out the sort of tasks involved in doing the job. For example, an applicant for a clerical post may be required to carry out tests involving word processing or the use of the telephone.

Fig. 5.4 Examples of intelligence tests

Appointment

AQA A AQA B
EDEXCEL
OCR A OCR B
WJEC
NICCEA

The contract of employment

Once the applicant has been selected by the interview panel and has accepted the position offered, a **contract of employment** is drawn up. This contract contains the following information.

CONTRACT OF EMPLOYMENT
job title . . . .

employer's name	employee's name ....
starting date	hours of work ....
pay and pay intervals	holidays and holiday pay ....
sickness and sickness pay	pension details ....
length of notice required	disciplinary rules ....

Fig. 5.5 A contract of employment

Ending the appointment

> The government provides a redundancy fund, and many firms have their own redundancy agreements providing better redundancy pay than the minimum given by law.

Employees may be made **redundant**. Redundancy occurs when their jobs are no longer needed by the firm, for example as a result of changes in work practice or production methods, or changes in demand for the firm's goods and services. Staff may receive some redundancy pay, the amount depending on factors such as their length of service, age and rate of pay.

An employee can be **dismissed** where there is a good reason to do so. Typical situations in which employees are dismissed include stealing the firm's goods, when their continued employment would be illegal (e.g. where a lorry driver has been banned from driving), and where their conduct at work deserves dismissal (such as continued drunkenness or violent behaviour). An employee will be given verbal warnings, followed by written warnings, before being dismissed. All employees have protection against **unfair dismissal**.

KEY POINT
The recruitment and selection process can be a long and expensive one, so HR Department staff need to be careful and thorough when employing people.

PROGRESS CHECK

1. List **three** external sources for obtaining staff.
2. Name **three** types of test that may be carried out at an interview.

2. Intelligence tests; personality tests; aptitude tests.
1. JobCentres; recruitment agencies; advertising in newspapers.

5.3 Training people

LEARNING SUMMARY

After studying this section you should be able to understand:

● *induction training*
● *internal training*
● *external training*

Induction training

AQA A   AQA B
EDEXCEL
OCR A   OCR B
WJEC
NICCEA

The Human Resources Department has the task of making sure that new employees start working efficiently as soon as possible. To do this, an **induction** training programme is set up. As employees become settled in their jobs, further training may be offered by Human Resources. This training will either be **internal** – run within the firm – or **external**, taking place outside the firm.

The purpose of induction training is to get the new employees to feel 'at home' as quickly as possible. By doing so, they settle in and soon start making a useful contribution to work. It also provides new employees with a feeling of 'being wanted', and so improves levels of morale.

A typical induction programme

Here is an example of a typical induction programme.

INDUCTION PROGRAMME FOR NEW STAFF		
DAY	ACTIVITY	VENUE and TIME
Monday:	Our company's history and present-day activities	Board Room: 10 am
	Tour of the company	Board Room: 11 am
	Lunch	Staff canteen: 1 pm
	The role of Human Resources in your development	Human Resources Dept, Interview room: 2.30 pm
	The work of your Department	Interview room: 3 pm
Tuesday:	Introduction to your Department	Department Manager's office: 9 am
	Meet your new colleagues	Department: 9.30 am

Fig. 5.6 An induction programme

Internal and external training

AQA A   AQA B
EDEXCEL
OCR   OCR
WJEC
NICCEA

Human Resources
may also organise
short courses and run
them on the firm's
premises.

Internal training

Also known as '**on-the-job**' training, this is the most popular form of training provided by firms. The employees learn as they work, the 'teacher' being the person currently doing the job or an instructor employed by Human Resources.

Because internal training usually takes place in the employees' normal place of work, it is **fully related to the firm's needs**, and also **quick and inexpensive to organise**. It does have the disadvantage that **the training is only as good as the trainers**, who may possess poor training skills and also find that their own work is delayed.

> **KEY POINT**
> Internal training can result in good, and bad, working practices being taught.

External training

This '**off-the-job**' training involves employees attending local colleges or other training providers, and studying to improve their skills. Since training specialists are employed, there should be **a high standard of training**. This form of training also **introduces new ideas and techniques** from outside into the firm and it is likely to be **more highly regarded by the trainees** if they are studying for a nationally recognised qualification.

External training may be **more expensive** than internal training (although no member of staff has to be released to train the employee), and is not devoted exclusively to the needs of the firm.

Government training schemes

The Department for Education and Employment nowadays organises a variety of training schemes: for example, the **New Deal** training initiative provides financial support for training and salary costs, and **Modern Apprenticeships** were established to provide apprentice training for young people.

> **KEY POINT**
> The cost for a firm of not training staff can be demotivated employees, a high labour turnover and a lack of competitiveness.

PROGRESS CHECK

1. Why do firms provide induction training for new employees?
2. State **two** advantages that internal training has over external training.

2. Related directly to the firm's requirements; inexpensive to organise and carry out.
1. To enable them to settle in quickly and to motivate them.

5.4 Motivation and job satisfaction

LEARNING SUMMARY

After studying this section you should be able to understand:

● *why people seek work*
● *two motivation theories*
● *how job satisfaction can be created*

Human needs and work

AQA A   AQA B
EDEXCEL
OCR   OCR
WJEC
NICCEA

There are many different occupations in the UK, and we have learnt how these occupations can be classified (page 16) into the different sectors of our economy. Regardless of the type of job, the new employee will hope to achieve some form of **job satisfaction**.

People seek employment for a number of reasons. **Pay** is an important motivator for many employees, but people also seem to want to work for other reasons as well. **Motivation** is important in business, because it identifies how satisfied or dissatisfied people are in their work. Employees who are highly motivated tend to work efficiently: if their level of motivation is low, output will suffer and labour disputes may also occur.

The work of Maslow and Herzberg

AQA A   AQA B
EDEXCEL
OCR   OCR
WJEC
NICCEA

Maslow and motivation

There have been many theories put forward in an attempt to explain why people want to work. An American psychologist, **Abraham Maslow**, identified a range of **human needs** that he believed people tried to satisfy. As one type of need became satisfied, another type of need would then be present. He placed these needs in a 'hierarchy': an order of importance.

BASIC
e.g. shelter

SAFETY

SOCIAL

EGO
e.g. job

SELF-FULFILMENT
Personal ambition

Fig. 5.7 Maslow's hierarchy

Fig 5.7 shows that Maslow believed there were five groups of needs.

1. The first, **basic**, needs are to do with survival and include the need for clothing, warmth and shelter. People also want these basic needs to be met in a business environment.
2. Once the basic needs are satisfied, people's **safety** needs must be met. A person needs to be safe from harm both at home and at work: a safe (secure) job is also important.
3. When the basic and safety needs are satisfied, an individual's **social** needs become important: people look for the friendship that comes from being part of a group, such as a group of workmates.
4. Once these three groups of needs are being satisfied, the need to achieve something personal then arises. People have **ego** needs to fulfil. These needs come from a desire for self-esteem, linked to having a job and to making a positive contribution to society.
5. The highest needs are the **self-fulfilment** ones. They involve some form of personal ambition: in the work situation, this could refer to finding great job satisfaction through doing work that includes a lot of responsibility or which is highly creative, and where its quality and importance is widely recognised.

The first three needs are sometimes referred to as 'lower' needs, and the top two are known as the 'higher' needs.

According to Maslow – and to most other theorists – **employers need to recognise that there is a range of needs that work must meet**. As a result, they should provide their employees with jobs that are satisfying in order for output to be at its most efficient.

> **KEY POINT**
>
> Maslow's theory highlights the importance of work to individuals, and offers some explanation of why unemployment is such a major problem for economies where employment is regarded as 'the norm'.

Herzberg and motivation

Another American psychologist, Frederick Herzberg, identified what he called **hygiene factors** in work. These are the basic, essential factors such as acceptable working conditions (e.g. safety, cleanliness, adequate rest breaks, control of noise) that form the foundation for having happy and well-motivated employees. Ignoring these hygiene factors will cause morale and motivation to fall, leading to lower output from an unhappy workforce.

Although hygiene factors need to be present at work, Herzberg argued that they do not, by themselves, motivate the employees. The **motivators** for employees include:

● **recognition** – having your efforts at work recognised by people
● **achievement** – the feeling of a 'job well done'
● **advancement** – such as actual (or possible) promotion
● **responsibility** – being given the responsibility to carry out jobs at work

>
>
> **KEY POINT**
>
> According to Herzberg these 'motivators' are the factors that employers should take into account when considering how best to motivate their staff.

Job satisfaction

AQA A   AQA B
EDEXCEL
OCR   OCR
WJEC
NICCEA

The 'caring professions', such as nursing, are examples of careers in which people are not motivated exclusively by pay, although recruitment into nursing (which is not highly paid) has proved difficult in recent years.

Staff in banks and building societies can often obtain mortgages and loans at favourable rates.

Different people have different ideas about what makes a job 'satisfying'. The ideas of Maslow and Herzberg give us some clues to those factors which lead people to enjoy their work.

Here are the major influences on job satisfaction.

1. The **pay level** for a job is important. High levels of pay allow employees to buy more material possessions: a high wage can also often compensate for unpleasant working conditions. Many employees will still accept a pay level lower than they could earn elsewhere, since pay is only one of a number of factors.

2. **Fringe benefits**, also known as 'perks', can influence the level of job satisfaction. Popular perks include company cars or subsidised travel, subsidised holidays, private health insurance, and non-contributory (free) pension schemes. Employees may be allowed to buy the company's goods at a discount, or to benefit from its services at discount rates.

3. The **working hours** may be attractive, or shift-work and 'unsocial hours' may be involved. The length of the working day, the number of holidays and the convenience of 'flexitime' working all influence the level of job satisfaction.

4. The **environment** also influences job satisfaction. This includes the level of noise, vibration or dust; the availability and quality of facilities such as canteens; and the degree and quality of heating and ventilation (e.g. whether there is air-conditioning).

Other factors influencing job satisfaction include the degree of **job security** and the presence of **friendly colleagues**.

KEY POINT These factors don't exist in isolation, but combine to give an overall level of satisfaction for a particular job.

PROGRESS CHECK

1. Name the five levels in Maslow's hierarchy of human needs.
2. State **three** influences on job satisfaction.

2. Pay rate; fringe benefits; working conditions.
1. Basic; safety; social; ego; self-fulfillment.

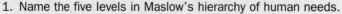

5.5 Paying people

LEARNING SUMMARY

After studying this section you should be able to understand:

● *wages and salaries, and how they are paid*
● *how pay is calculated*

Wages and salaries

AQA A   AQA B
EDEXCEL
OCR   OCR
WJEC
NICCEA

> Profit is often described as 'the reward for the entrepreneur', since it is the reward for taking risk.

Employees normally earn either a wage or a salary, as a **reward** for their labour. Fig. 5.8 shows us the typical differences between a 'waged' employee and a 'salaried' employee.

	TYPE OF PAY	
Wage	TYPE OF PAY	Salary
Manual	TYPICAL WORK	Clerical
Weekly	FREQUENCY OF PAYMENT	Monthly
Likely to receive payment for overtime	NATURE OF PAY	Fixed annual sum: often no overtime paid

Fig. 5.8 Wages and salaries

Different groups of workers in the same firm, and in different occupations in the UK, will have different pay levels.

1. One reason why doctors, accountants, lawyers and many other 'professionals' normally receive high salaries is due to the **level of qualifications** and **length of training** they need.
2. Pay also varies depending on where we are employed in the UK economy: **private sector** pay tends to be higher than that in the **public sector**.
3. Another reason is based on the laws of **supply and demand**. People with skills that are scarce (there are few of them supplying these skills) but which are in great demand, will receive very high pay.
4. Work varies according to the **degree of danger or discomfort** involved: people employed in more dangerous or uncomfortable occupations (e.g. oil rig workers) may receive higher pay as a result.
5. The **location of the work** also influences pay levels. For example, people living in London and South-East England may receive an extra 'London weighting' in their pay, because the higher living costs mean that employees have to be attracted to (or encouraged to stay in) the area by being offered higher pay rates.
6. **Trade unions** can influence pay rates: many non-union occupations traditionally receive low rates of pay.

> Some FA Premiership footballers receive more in a week than most people earn in a year: there is a high demand for their skills.

> The UK now has a national minimum wage. Established in April 1999, at that time it was set at £3.60 per hour. It has since increased.

KEY POINT

> Different levels of pay in an economy are called wage differentials.

Payment systems

AQA A   AQA B
EDEXCEL
OCR   OCR
WJEC
NICCEA

There are a number of different ways of calculating and paying employees.

Flat rate

Salaries are normally paid at a **fixed rate**: one-twelfth of the annual salary figure is paid into the employee's bank account. Many wages are also paid at a set weekly rate. The advantage to the firm is that the individual's pay – and therefore the total wage bill – is easily calculated; the disadvantage is that employees don't have a financial incentive to work harder.

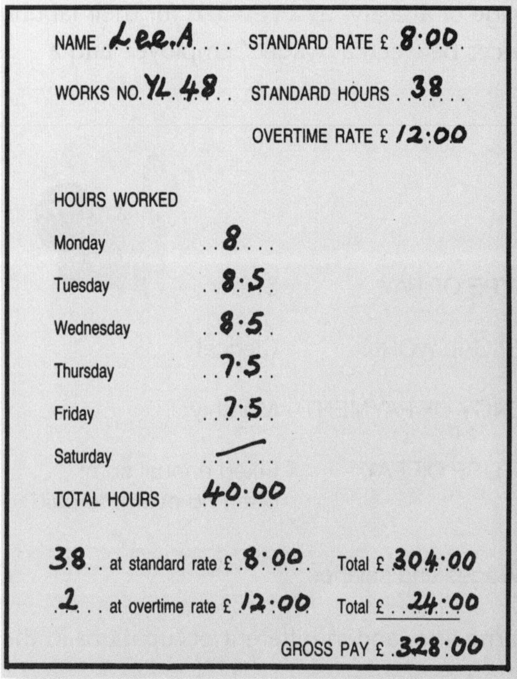

Time rate

Employees are paid a **set amount per hour** for every hour worked. After a given number of hours have been worked, the employee may be paid at **overtime** rates: 'time and a third', 'time and a half' and 'double time' are common overtime rates. Fig. 5.9 is an example of how an employee's wages are calculated using a time rate system. The advantage to firms of this system is that extra work (overtime) is encouraged through extra pay, but the total wages bill is more difficult to estimate, and to calculate because a 'clocking in and clocking off' system must be used.

```
NAME ..Lee.A....   STANDARD RATE £ .8:00.

WORKS NO. YL.48..  STANDARD HOURS ..38...

                   OVERTIME RATE £ /2:00


HOURS WORKED

Monday        ..8...

Tuesday       ..8:5.

Wednesday     .8:5.

Thursday      ..7:5..

Friday        ..7:5..

Saturday      ...—...

TOTAL HOURS   40.00


38.. at standard rate £ .8:00.  Total £ 304.00

.2... at overtime rate £ /2:00   Total £ ..24.00

                GROSS PAY £ .328:00
```

Fig. 5.9 Time rate calculation

Piece rate

With piece rate, the items made must be of an acceptable quality for payment to be received.

Employees making items are paid **an agreed amount for each item made**. The items must be of an acceptable quality for pay to be received. Part of their wages may be at a flat rate, with the rest on a piece rate basis. A popular variation is where sales staff receive **commission** for each sale they make: the commission may also be supported by 'basic' (flat-rate) pay.

Employees are encouraged to work hard, since higher output means higher pay, and efficient and hard-working employees receive more pay than inefficient staff. However, the quality of the output may suffer due to employees rushing their work, and so more quality control supervision becomes necessary.

Bonuses and profit-sharing schemes

Employees may receive bonuses during the year, such as just before Christmas. The firm may operate a **merit bonus** scheme, in which staff exceeding production or selling targets – or, with office staff, those employees regarded as being most efficient – receive a bonus or a higher-than-average pay increase. Bonuses can, therefore, encourage loyalty amongst staff, as well as improving production and sales by setting targets linked to a financial reward. A bonus system can, however, lead to disputes, since the level of bonus to be awarded can be difficult to calculate.

Many firms now have an agreement with the workforce to **share out part of the profits** between the employees as a form of bonus. A company's **shares** may also be distributed. These schemes have the advantage of making staff feel a part of the firm because they are sharing directly in the profits they have helped create.

'It is good to see that over 70 000 of our staff are now shareholders and 106 000 are eligible for profit sharing this year ...' (Source: Tesco plc annual review, 1999)

'Employees of group companies are encouraged to participate in the success of the business through incentive and share option schemes.' (Source: PizzaExpress plc annual report, 1999)

Fig. 5.10 Companies using profit-sharing and share incentive schemes

KEY POINT The method of payment depends mainly on the type of work done, although more and more firms nowadays recognise the value of 'employee-share' schemes such as share ownership.

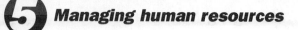

Gross pay and net pay

AQA A   AQA B
EDEXCEL
OCR A   OCR B
WJEC
NICCEA

Fig. 5.9 shows how a person's pay is calculated on a time rate basis. The total wage of £328 is the employee's gross pay, but the amount of 'take-home' pay is less. There are a series of **deductions** – some voluntary, some compulsory – before the employee receives net pay.

CODE NO.	PAY NO.	NAME	N.I. NO.	Month	PAY ADVICE
374L	0113611	V. HODGSON	YL324892A	DEC.	

CUMULATIVE INFORMATION		PAY		DEDUCTIONS	
PAY TO DATE	**SUP'N to DATE**	BASIC	925.00	INCOME TAX	174.50
8471.25	540.75	OVERTIME	14.00	NAT. INS.	61.50
TAX TO DATE	**N.I. TO DATE**	OTHER		SUPERAN.	58.00
1566.50	576.60			OTHER	2.00
GROSS PAY	939.00				
TOTAL DEDUCTIONS	296.00				
NET PAY	643.00	TOTAL	939.00	TOTAL	296.00

Fig. 5.11 A payslip

Information on the payslip

- **Tax code number.** The 'PAYE' (**pay as you earn**) method is normally used to collect income tax. All employees can earn so much free of tax, and their tax code number helps the firm calculate the correct tax.
- **Deductions.** As well as tax, employees pay **national insurance** towards the cost of the State retirement pension and the National Health Service. Another common deduction is **superannuation**, i.e. payment into a pension scheme. Other deductions may include **trade union subscriptions** and 'SAYE' (**save as you earn**) schemes.

PROGRESS CHECK

1. State **two** differences between a wage and a salary.
2. List **four** payment systems.

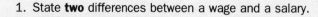

2. Time rate; flat rate; piece rate; bonuses.

1. Wages are paid weekly, salaries monthly; wages associated with manual work, salaries with 'office'.

5.6 Labour relations

After studying this section you should be able to understand:

● **trade unions**
● **employers' associations**
● **disputes, and how they can be resolved**

Trade unions

AQA A   AQA B
EDEXCEL
OCR A   OCR B
WJEC
NICCEA

The nature of trade unions

The relationship between employer and employee has been described as a 'master and servant' one. Because individual employees are not in a very powerful position, they have often acted together as a single unit – a **union** – to protect their interests at work.

In recent years, the trend has been for **trade union membership to fall**, both in total and as a percentage of the UK's workforce. Reasons for this include:

● a rise in temporary or part-time jobs (these employees are less likely to join unions)
● a fall in the number of manufacturing-based jobs, where union membership was traditionally very high

Trade union membership fell from about 13 million in 1979 to about 8 million in 2000.

Another important trend has been for unions to **merge and grow in size**: about two-thirds of union members belong to the ten largest unions. An example is the Amalgamated Engineering and Electrical Union (the AEEU), with about 750 000 employees in 2000, which planned to merge with the Manufacturing Science Finance Union (MSF), with over 400 000 members. We still find small unions, such as the Professional Footballers' Association (the PFA) with about 2000 members.

Percentage of all employees, Autumn 1998							
	Manual			Non-manual			All
	males	females	total	males	females	total	employees
England	33	21	29	26	30	28	28
Wales	43	28	37	43	45	44	41
Scotland	37	27	33	34	39	37	35
Northern Ireland	38	34	37	42	43	43	40
UK	**34**	**22**	**30**	**28**	**31**	**30**	**30**

Fig. 5.12 UK trade union membership

Why do people join unions? These reasons are normally given, in order of importance (the source is the *British Social Attitude Survey*):

● to protect our **jobs**
● to improve our **working conditions**

- to improve **pay**
- to have **more say** over management's long-term plans

Types of trade union

We normally separate the 'blue-collar' unions into three types – **craft**, **industrial** and **general** – and we also recognise a fourth type, the '**white-collar**' union.

- **Craft unions** were originally set up to control entrants to particular skilled occupations (crafts). Some of these unions are very small, and one company may find a number of them representing its workforce: this can make negotiations difficult. Examples include the Musicians' Union (MU) with 30 000 members in the year 2000, and CATU, the Ceramic and Allied Trades Union which had about 19 000 members in 2000.
- An **industrial union** contains most of the workers in that industry, and managers tend to find negotiations are more straightforward when dealing with only one union. The retail trade's USDAW (Union of Shop, Distributive and Allied Workers), which had about 300 000 members in 2000, is a good illustration.
- **General unions** are often very large, and may contain high proportions of semi-skilled and unskilled workers. Their members come from different industries. The large size of the union and the wide range of interests it represents can create difficulties for the union. UNISON, which had about 1.25 million members in the year 2000, is a general union for public sector employees in local government, health care, power supply, transport, and further and higher education administration.
- **White-collar unions** contain clerical and professional staff. Examples include the National Union of Teachers, which had about 200 000 members in the year 2000.

These groupings are being affected by changes in our economy.

Recent developments include the company union (the company has its own union), and single-union agreements – a firm agrees that only one union will represent its staff.

 KEY POINT White-collar unions have grown in size and importance in recent years.

The **structure** of the larger unions is often very similar. They have a **head office**, where the administration and the various **specialist staff** (e.g. specialising in employment law) are based. There may also be a number of **regional offices**. At a **local level**, the **shop steward** and/or other union officials help organise the union by arranging meetings with members, and then represent the members' views when they negotiate with management.

Aims of trade unions

All unions carry out activities to benefit their members, but they are subject to legal controls (see Chapter 4). We can summarise their main aims as follows.

1. To **negotiate with employers**. This bargaining is mainly to do with pay and bonuses, hours, working conditions, and pensions. Unions are interested in **job satisfaction**, and will negotiate concerning **job security**. **Collective bargaining** is the normal way that pay and conditions are agreed, with union officials representing groups of workers.

2. To **protect their members** against unfair dismissal, possible lay-offs and redundancy. Part-time workers may also be represented by the union, and protected: a union may also have to fight to give members the rights to which they are entitled, for equal pay and equal treatment for women, and against other forms of discrimination.

3. To **advise and represent** their members. Unions often provide personal support, and legal advice on problems at work. members having work-based accidents can be represented by union officials.

4. To **influence others**. Unions seek to influence employers, employer organisations and the government in order to benefit their members.

Unions win over £300 million each year as compensation for members who suffer injuries, or discrimination at work.

Benefits of union membership

Staff joining a trade union will pay a subscription. For this, they receive a number of benefits from their union membership.

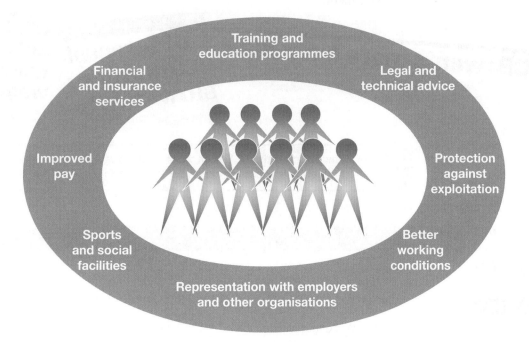

Fig. 5.13 Benefits of trade union membership

Controlling trade unions

Trade union power came under attack from the government in the 1980s. The Acts that were passed required the main union officers to be elected by a secret ballot, and strike action must also be authorised by secret ballots.

The TUC also has an office in Brussels, to keep in close touch with EU developments.

The Trades Union Congress (TUC)

In the same way that it helps individuals to get together and form a union, it can be in the joint interest of unions to do the same. The **TUC** is the central body where unions come together to discuss matters affecting them all. Most unions are **affiliated** to – members of – the TUC. As a result, the TUC acts as the unions' 'voice' when discussing employment issues with the government or employer associations. The TUC helps settle union disputes, and has a programme of union education.

Employers' organisations

AQA A   AQA B
EDEXCEL
OCR A   OCR B
WJEC
NICCEA

> The CBI is a good illustration of a pressure group.

These associations act as the employer equivalent of unions. The **Confederation of British Industry** (the CBI) was founded in 1965 and is the major employers' association. It represents all levels and types of industry, in both private and public sectors. The CBI will negotiate with the TUC on employment law and issues, and – like the TUC – will try to persuade the government to carry out policies that are in the interests of its members. It represents, directly and indirectly, about 250 000 companies.

Other employer organisations include **trade associations** and other bodies existing to support businesses in their special areas. Examples include the Road Haulage Association and the Society of Motor Manufacturers and Traders. Local **chambers of commerce** also support local firms, by providing advice and assistance, and are an important link between local firms and local and central government.

CBI wants more from Blair

ness Editor Carl Jones.   *Email: CJones@shro*

CBI forecast economy to slow down

CBI hits out over minimum wage

Fig. 5.14 Involvement of the CBI

KEY POINT
The TUC and the CBI often work closely together because it is in both organisations' interests for the economy to become stronger.

Disputes

AQA A   AQA B
EDEXCEL
OCR A   OCR B
WJEC
NICCEA

> Many more days are lost through illness than through strike action.

In recent years, days lost to industrial disputes have fallen, but collective bargaining doesn't always succeed, and disputes can still occur.

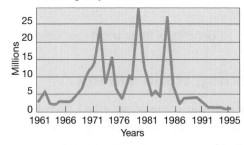

Working days lost, UK

Days lost per 1000 employees		
1996	**1997**	**1998**
57	10	12

Fig. 5.15 Working days lost to labour disputes (Source: ONS)

A union may take different forms of industrial action.

- With **overtime bans**, the union instructs its members not to work overtime: this leads to falling output and puts pressure on the employer to agree to the union's demands.
- In a **work-to-rule**, employees follow the 'rule book' very closely, which can slow down or even halt production.
- A **go-slow** occurs when members carry out their work more slowly than normal: this also reduces output.

- Employees may resort to **sit-ins**, refusing to leave the premises and occupying them in an attempt to make sure that goods neither enter nor leave the firm. Most sit-ins take place when there is a threat to close the business.

Strikes

The last resort is for union members to go on strike and **withdraw their labour**. This isn't a popular strategy with unions, because members lose pay, there may be legal issues and problems, and it may even result in the firm closing with employees losing their jobs.

> **An important recent trend has been for unions to make 'sweetheart deals' with companies, effectively giving up the right to strike in return for single union recognition and increased consultation.**

Nowadays strikes tend to be **official**, with the union having to consult with, and ballot, its members before any strike action can be taken. **Unofficial** 'wildcat' strikes are less common, but may still occur. To make the strike more effective, union members **picket** the firm to discourage others from crossing their picket line and entering the firm's premises.

Resolving the dispute

The dispute may be resolved – ended – by the action of one or both of the opposing parties. The government may also put some pressure on the parties to end the dispute.

If the dispute carries on for some time, **ACAS** – the Advisory, Conciliation and Arbitration Service – may become involved. ACAS was set up in 1975 to improve industrial relations. It is independent from both employers and unions, and offers two main services.

> **Other services offered by ACAS include publishing guidelines and 'codes of practice' on industrial relations.**

1. **Conciliation**. An ACAS official talks to both sides to find areas of 'common ground', which then form the basis for further negotiations.
2. **Arbitration**. If both sides agree, their dispute 'goes to arbitration'. ACAS provides an independent third party to listen to the points made, and offers a settlement (the employer and the union, by going to arbitration, have agreed to accept whatever settlement is offered).

> 'To improve the performance and effectiveness of organisations by providing an independent and impartial service to prevent and resolve disputes and to build harmonious relationships at work.'

Fig. 5.16 The mission statement of ACAS

PROGRESS CHECK

1. Identify **four** aims of trade unions.
2. List **four** forms of industrial action that union members may take.

1. Negotiate with employers; protect members; advise and represent members; influence others.
2. Go-slows; overtime bans; working to rule; strikes.

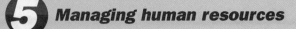

Sample GCSE questions

This question is about recruiting and selecting staff.

1. Candy Box Ltd. is a small company that specialises in the production of chocolates. They need to recruit a new Personal Secretary to the Managing Director. The Human Resources department has been told to draw up a job description and a person specification for the post and to place a job advertisement in the Belfast Telegraph.

(a) What type of production is Candy Box involved in? **(1)**

Candy Box is a manufacturer so it is Secondary production.

(b) What are the other **two** types of production? **(2)**

Primary and tertiary.

(c) Why is a job description drawn up? **(2)**

It is drawn up so that people can see what the job involves. ◄

> *This is rather vague as an answer: you need to give specific examples such as 'it outlines the duties and responsibilities of the post', and 'it helps the applicant see exactly what is involved'.*

(d) Name and explain any **two** pieces of information which should appear in the job description for a Personal Secretary. **(4)**

The hours of work: when the person has to be there (start and finish times). The pay (how much each week). ◄

> *Good examples (though an annual, rather than a weekly, salary is more likely to be stated).*

(e) How, other than through newspapers, could the firm have advertised this post? **(2)**

The firm could have advertised through the local Job Centre because people living locally will have the skills needed. ◄

> *Only one example is given: you should support this with another.*

(f) Why is it important to prepare a person specification for this job? **(4)**

So that Candy Box can see if the applicants are OK for the post. ◄

> *Terms such as 'OK for the post' are vague: you should point out e.g that the person spec helps the company to shortlist, and that it can be used in the interview.*

(g) Explain why Candy Box would want to interview the candidates. **(2)**

So that they could talk to the candidates to see if they are any good at the job of Personal Secretary. ◄

> *Again, the phrase 'to see if they are any good' is vague.*

(h) (i) Describe **two** ways, other than interview, which Candy Box could use to select a person for the job. **(4)**

    (ii) Explain how government legislation could affect Candy Box's recruitment procedures. **(4)**

(i) Candy Box could use an employment agency to get them a suitable person. Candy Box could use tests to make sure the person can do the job. ◄

> *These agencies recruit, not select, people. You should mention the various tests that can be used in selection.*

(ii) Government legislation is when laws are passed. Laws to do with employing people protect against race, sex and disability discrimination so that Candy Box will be fair and legal when it comes to employing people. ◄

> *This is quite a good answer, because it mentions three important areas (race, sex and disability).*

CCEA Foundation Tier, 2000

Exam practice questions

1. Read the newspaper item below and answer the questions which follow.

Strike Threatens Bag Plant

The Transport and General Workers Union have announced that, following a ballot, fifty members who work at Gripabag will be on indefinite strike from next week. Gripabag manufactures sports bags for a variety of branded sports goods retailers. The shop steward at the factory, Mr Dave Jenks, said that the company intended to install new machinery without consulting the union about the effects on jobs and working practices. The Managing Director of Gripabag, Mrs Helen Johnson, has commented that the action by the workers was being taken before they appreciated the benefits that the new machines will provide for the firm and for their long-term job prospects. Negotiations with the unions would be held as soon as they could be arranged. She was confident that the strike would not take place.

(a) Apart from attempting to protect jobs, briefly describe **two** other ways in which trades unions help their members. **(3)**

....

....

(b) Workers at Gripabag are paid £7 per hour for a forty hour week and overtime is paid at time and a half. Calculate the wages paid if fifty hours are worked in a particular week. (Show your workings.) **(3)**

....

....

(c) Explain why the new machines are likely to reduce jobs at Gripabag. **(4)**

....

....

(d) Evaluate Mrs Helen Johnson's comment that the new machines will provide benefits for the firm and long-term job prospects for the employees. **(8)**

....

....

....

....

WJEC Specimen Paper 1

Exam practice questions

2. Garfield Print uses computers to design items such as wedding stationery, posters and catalogues for its customers. It is going to recruit a new employee to design posters and catalogues using the latest computer technology. Each applicant has been asked to send a curriculum vitae (CV) and a letter of application prepared on a computer.

(a) (i) What is a curriculum vitae? (2)

....

(ii) In selecting for this particular job, explain why you think Garfield Print wants applications done on a computer to help it select the new employee. (2)

....

Garfield Print has received ten applications and has decided to use testing as another way of selecting the person for the job.

(b) (i) Describe **two** methods by which Garfield Print could test the applicants for the job. (4)

....

(ii) Select **one** of these methods and explain what Garfield Print can find out from this test. (2)

....

Garfield Print has decided to interview five applicants.

(c) Why do you think an interview is a good way to make the final selection of the new employee? (4)

....

(d) (i) What is the purpose of a contract of employment? (2)

....

(ii) State **four** items which would be contained in the contract of employment. (4)

....

Garfield Print employs 20 people and has a flat management structure.

(e) (i) Explain **two** reasons why the owners of Garfield Print may prefer to have a flat management structure. (4)

....

(ii) What is the name given to the **other** type of management structure which Garfield Print could use? (1)

....

6 Finance and accounting

The following topics are included in this chapter:

- **Finance for business**
- **Costs**
- **Forecasting and budgeting**
- **Financial accounting**
- **Interpreting accounts**

6.1 Finance for business

LEARNING SUMMARY

After studying this section you should be able to understand:

- **why firms need finance**
- **the main types of internal and external finance available**
- **limited company shares and debentures**

Why businesses need finance

AQA A   AQA B
EDEXCEL
OCR A   OCR B
WJEC
NICCEA

Entrepreneurs – the business decision-makers – need money to start their businesses. They have to buy or hire the **assets** that they need to make or supply their goods and services.

Once set up, a firm has to meet its short-term debts which come from trading activities such as buying stock on credit. This short-term finance is known as the firm's **working capital** (page 110). Any firm without enough working capital will have problems surviving. It can't take advantage of cost-saving discounts, since it doesn't have the cash available: its **creditors** (suppliers on credit) could demand payment of the money they're owed, and they could even take legal action, forcing the firm to close down and sell off its assets to meet these debts.

Firms also need **long-term capital** so they can expand. There are many sources of long-term capital: personal savings for sole traders and shares in limited companies are two well-known examples.

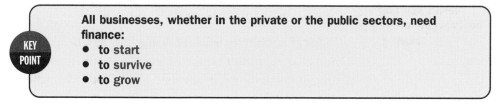

KEY POINT

All businesses, whether in the private or the public sectors, need finance:
- to start
- to survive
- to grow

Sources of finance for the private sector

Our main private sector organisations – sole traders, partnerships and limited companies – can use both internal and external sources of finance. These firms can raise funds (finance) **internally** by:

- **retaining and using profits** – some profits are held back, not withdrawn, spent by the sole traders/partners or 'spent' in the form of shareholders' dividends, but used to develop the business
- **selling assets** – assets that are no longer required
- **using trade credit** – the owners may take advantage of the credit offered to them by their suppliers, and also reduce the credit periods they offer to their own customers (getting more money in quickly, which is a source of finance)
- **investing any surplus cash** – the interest on this investment being a source of finance
- **reducing stocks held** – so that cash is released and not 'tied up' in these stocks

These private sector firms can also get finance from **external** sources. The main examples are:

- **personal savings**
- **borrowing** from family or friends
- **issuing shares** (by limited companies)
- **loans and mortgages** from banks, building societies and other financial organisations, or from central and local government
- **using finance houses**, e.g. to lease (rent) equipment such as photocopiers, or using credit sale or hire purchase to buy assets
- **overdrafts** from banks, where the firm can – by arranging with the bank – withdraw more money than it has in its account
- **factoring debts** – the firm can sell its debts to a debt factor company, receiving most of the debt's value immediately rather than having to wait for the full debt to be paid

PROD. CODE	QUANTITY AND DESCRIPTION	UNIT PRICE £ p	TOTAL £ p
EV8	10 'Foxy' cuddly toys	2 50	25 00
TD2	12 'Tina' dolls	12 00	144 00

EVF Co Ltd
Highbridge Road, Wellington, Somerset TA1 2ER
Telephone (01952) 459741 Fax (01952) 459842

To: Laura's Stores Ltd
Taunton Road
Burnham-on-Sea
Somerset LS7 8EF
Date: 19.8.97
Order No.: 160180

Less: Trade discount 10% — 169 00 / 16 90
152 10
Value Added Tax at 17½% — 26 62
TOTAL DUE 178 72
Terms: 2½% 28 days E&OE
VAT Reg. 403-8871-988

Fig. 6.1 A trade credit document (an invoice)

The larger amounts of finance tend to come from external, not internal, sources.

Sources of finance for the public sector

Two of the main types of business organisation in our public sector are public corporations (page 43) and local authority undertakings (page 44).

Public corporations are financed mainly through **taxes**, and by either **borrowing** from the Treasury or by using any profits the corporation makes through its trading activities.

A **local authority undertaking** may also be financed by borrowing (from the local authority) or using profits from any trading it carries out, and through the authority raising income (e.g. from local Council tax) and giving a grant to the undertaking.

The Treasury is the UK Government department that controls government spending.

Shares and debentures

The most important source of finance for the larger firms – limited companies – in the private sector comes from issuing shares and debentures.

- **Shares** tell us that their holders own a 'share' of the company. A **public limited company** (plc: page 36) is allowed to sell its shares to the general public, by issuing a prospectus; afterwards, its 'second-hand' shares are traded on the stock exchange. A **private limited company** ('Ltd.': page 36) must sell its shares privately: these cannot be bought and sold on the stock exchange.
- **Debentures** (long-term loans) may be issued: the lenders receive interest, and will have their capital (loan) paid back at some time in the future.

> **'Debenture' is the name of the document issued to the lenders of this long-term loan.**

Types of shares

Companies issue two main types of share: ordinary and preference.

Ordinary shares allow their holders to **vote** at company meetings. This makes an ordinary shareholder an **owner** of the company. The rate of **dividend** – the payment made to the shareholders – depends on company profits: it is a **variable** rate. Ordinary shareholders are also the **last to be paid** out of net profit, and so they face the risk of not receiving any dividend if profits are low. They are also the **last to have their capital repaid** if the company is 'wound up'.

> **Ordinary shares are also known as 'equity' or 'equities'.**

Preference shares, unlike ordinary ones, don't usually give their holders the right to vote at company meetings. The preference shareholders receive **priority** over ordinary shareholders when it comes to paying dividend and repaying capital. The preference dividend is **fixed** and, because it is paid before the ordinary dividend, stands more chance of being paid. Some preference shares are **cumulative** – this means that if profits in one year are too low to pay the preference dividend, the amount owing to the shareholders is carried forward to future years and will be paid if future profits are high enough.

Preference shares are therefore a **safer investment** than ordinary shares, but they will not receive high returns when profits are high – their dividend stays at the fixed amount.

	Ordinary	Preference
voting rights?	normally one vote per share	usually non-voting
dividend payment?	variable (high or low depending on profits)	fixed, regardless of profit level
capital repaid?	paid after preference; repaid last	paid before ordinary; repaid before ordinary

Fig. 6.2 Ordinary and preference shares

> **KEY POINT** Ordinary shares are regarded as more of a 'gamble' than preference shares.

Debentures

Debentures are also named **loan stock** and are a long-term loan to a company. The debenture holders are **creditors** of the company, and not owners (unlike shareholders). The loan is normally **secured** against company assets: if the company cannot repay the loan, the debenture holder has the right to sell the asset to recover the debt owed.

In return for this loan, the debenture holder receives a **fixed rate of interest** on the loan: this payment must be made by the company, whether it is making a profit or a loss. Like other loans, a debenture loan will have to be repaid in the future.

	Shareholders	Debenture holders
status?	owners of the company	lenders to the company
reward?	dividend, paid out of business expense	interest, paid whether or not the company makes a profit
repayment?	not normally repaid, unless the company is wound up	normally repayable at a future date: if company is wound up; repaid before shareholders

Fig. 6.3 Shareholders and debenture holders

KEY POINT Debenture interest is a normal business expense, and not paid out of the company's net profits.

How the source of finance is chosen

AQA A AQA B
EDEXCEL
OCR A OCR B
WJEC
NICCEA

Firms don't normally rely on one source of long-term finance, and there is usually a range of sources from which they can choose. The main factors influencing which source is chosen are shown in Fig. 6.4.

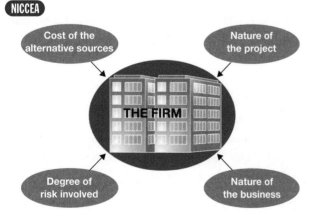

Fig. 6.4 Factors influencing the source of finance chosen

Firms often need extra finance for new projects (e.g. new products being planned, made and sold). The **nature of a project** may determine the source of finance. For example, long-term projects need injections of finance at different points in time, so a company may make several share issues or take out a series of loans; short-term projects are more likely to be financed by bank loans. Companies with projects needing a lot of highly technological equipment may choose to lease (rather than buy) these items, to ensure they keep using the most up-to-date equipment.

Shares are a good example of finance available only to limited companies.

The **nature of the business** also influences the source of finance. Some sources – such as shares – are only available to certain forms of business ownership. Firms in **high-risk** areas, and smaller firms, may find their sources of finance are restricted, and that the **cost of finance** – the rate of interest charged – is higher than average.

PROGRESS CHECK

1. State the difference between internal and external sources of finance.
2. Identify **two** differences between:
   (a) ordinary and preference shares;
   (b) shares and debentures.

1. Internal sources come from within the organisation; external are supplied from outside.
2. (a) Dividend (variable) ordinary; fixed preference); vote (ordinary yes; preference no)
   (b) Owners (shareholders) and lenders (debenture holders); dividend (shares) and interest (debentures)

6.2 Costs

LEARNING SUMMARY

After studying this section you should be able to understand:

- *how costs can be classified in different ways*
- *the construction and use of break-even charts*

Costs of production

AQA A AQA B
EDEXCEL
OCR A OCR B
WJEC
NICCEA

Efficient, large-scale production can bring a number of **economies of scale** (page 148) for a firm. But however efficient a firm is at producing its goods (or services), it will still have to meet various costs of production. Fig. 6.5 illustrates the costs.

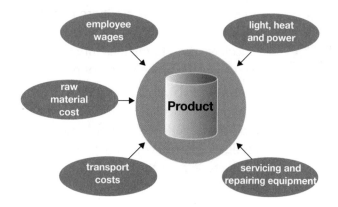

Fig. 6.5 Typical costs of production

We can classify these costs under different headings, to help **analyse** and **control** them. One type of cost we've already considered is **opportunity cost** (page 10), where the cost of doing something is measured by what else has to be given up in order to do it. For example, the opportunity cost for a toy producer which is bringing out a new battery-powered car might be a range of toy furniture for a doll's house: there aren't enough resources (such as capital, equipment and skilled staff) for the producer to make both.

KEY POINT

The different types of cost apply not only to production ('factory' costs), but also to administration, and to selling and distribution ('office' costs).

Fixed and variable costs

We can separate the total costs of a firm into those that are **fixed** and those that are **variable**. One reason for carrying out this analysis is so that we can undertake **break-even** calculations (page 103).

- **Fixed costs don't change as output changes**. Examples include factory and office rent, office salaries (they don't depend on the number of items produced), and insurance premiums, e.g. for the firm's vehicles. These costs don't change if the factory is working at full capacity, or if it is closed.

 KEY POINT — Fixed costs may change over a period of time – insurance premiums may go up, staff salaries will increase, and factory rent may rise – but they don't change in the short term as the firm's output changes.

- **Variable costs change as output changes**. These costs result from a firm's production, and therefore change as the output level changes. Examples include the costs of raw materials used to make the products, and 'piece-work' wages where workers are paid by the number of items they make.

In reality, the distinction between fixed and variable isn't so straightforward. Many costs are **semi-variable**, containing elements that are fixed and variable. For example, a factory's power costs may carry a fixed 'standing charge' that must be paid regardless of how much power is used, and a (variable) charge per unit of power used.

Direct and indirect costs

> Direct costs are often variable, and indirect costs are usually fixed in nature.

A firm's **direct costs** are those costs that can be **directly linked to particular product lines**. Examples include the costs of running the machinery used to manufacture the products, the cost of raw materials used in the product, and the wages of production workers.

Indirect costs are also known as **overheads**: these are shared between the different product lines and **do not relate to one particular product line**. Examples include the cost of company stationery used for all the company's products and services, salaries of office staff who are involved with all company products, and office and factory rent. The firm's management will want to know not only total costs (to calculate total profit), but also the costs of making individual product lines to calculate their profitability so that decisions can be made (e.g. about the price to charge for each product). In practice, the firm's accountant will **apportion** – share out – indirect costs to the different product lines, e.g. by sharing factory rent on the basis of the floor space taken by each product line.

Average and marginal costs

Economies of scale bring lower unit costs (cost per item made). This **average cost of production** is found by dividing total cost by total output. The **marginal cost** of a product is the **cost of making that individual product**. This probably won't work out to be the same as the average cost, because of the way that fixed costs are distributed across the number made.

For example:

- total fixed costs are £3000; variable costs are £100 per item made
- average cost of making one item =   £3100 / 1 = £3100
- average cost of making two items =   £3200 / 2 = £1600
- average cost to make three items =   £3300 / 3 = £1100

The marginal cost of the second and third items is, however, only £100 each.

> There is a close link between marginal costs and variable costs.

> **KEY POINT**
> The firm's managers find this information valuable, for example when deciding whether to take on a new order, and what price they can charge for that new order.

Standard costs

The use of standard costs is an attempt to calculate **what it should cost** to make something. Staff calculate the expected costs for each item or task making up the finished product or service, and they can then compare the 'should cost' with **what it has cost** to make the product or to supply the service.

What it SHOULD cost   What it DOES cost

Fig. 6.6 Checking standard costs against actual costs

Any difference between what it should cost and what it has cost in terms of materials, labour and overheads is called a **variance**. Management can analyse the variances between the standard cost of production and the actual cost of production, coming to conclusions about whether:

- more or less material than expected has been used
- the overall cost of material is more or less than expected
- labour is more or less efficient than expected
- labour is more or less expensive than expected
- production overheads are being recovered by charging a high enough price

> When managers check and act upon variances (differences), this is known as management by exception.

Break-even analysis

The break-even point for a firm is found where **total costs equal total revenues**. At this point the firm is making neither a profit nor a loss. The break-even point is particularly important to a firm, because it is after this point of output that it starts to make a profit.

> **KEY POINT**
> Break-even analysis uses fixed and variable costs to calculate the break-even point and show this on a graph.

Constructing the break-even chart

To do this, we need information on the firm's fixed costs, variable costs and selling price. We then plot the results on a graph that has pounds (£, costs and revenue) on the vertical axis and production/output on the horizontal axis.

- **Fixed cost (FC) line**. We'll assume a company's fixed costs total £10 000. The fixed cost line is plotted as a straight line which starts at the £10 000 point on the vertical axis and runs parallel to the horizontal axis (because fixed costs stay constant at £10 000). Fig. 6.7 shows this break-even chart, and the fixed cost line is labelled.

- **Variable cost (VC) line**. The firm's variable costs are 50p per unit. If output is planned at 5000 units, the total variable costs will be £2500 (5000 x 50p). We can plot this line on the chart. It starts where the fixed cost line meets the vertical axis: at this point, zero output, the variable cost is also zero. At the other end of the line – the 5000 output point – the gap between the fixed costs and the variable costs is £2500 (the total variable costs at this output).

- **Total costs (TC)**. Total Cost = Fixed Cost + Variable Cost. The variable cost line in Fig. 6.7 therefore also represents the firm's TC line. Total costs at the maximum output of 5000 units are £12 500: i.e. £10 000 FC + £2500 VC.

- **Total revenue (TR) line**. The TR line can be plotted. If the firm's selling price for its product is £3.00, the total revenue at the maximum output will be £15 000 (£3 x 5000). We can draw the TR line by joining this point on the graph to the zero point where the two axes meet (because at an output of zero, revenue is also zero).

- **Break-even point**. The firm's break-even point is where the TR and TC lines cross. A line drawn from this point down to the output axis shows that 4000 units represents the **break-even level of output**. Selling over 4000 units will give the firm a profit: the triangle below it, representing sales and output under 4000, is the area of loss.

- **Margin of safety**. If the firm sells 5000 units, its margin of safety lies between 5000 and the break-even point: it knows that its sales can fall to 4000 before it starts making a loss.

> Remember examples of fixed costs (e.g. rent, office salaries) and variable costs (e.g. raw materials, production wages).

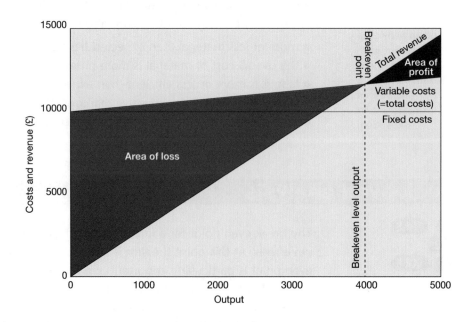

Fig. 6.7 Break-even chart

The profit or loss at all levels of output can be read from the chart. For example, at output and sales of 4500, the firm's TR line shows £13 500 and the TC line reads £12 250. The gap between these two lines – the firm's profit, since TR is (literally) above TC – is £1250.

Calculating the break-even point

A firm's management is interested in the amount of **contribution** a product makes to its fixed costs. These fixed costs must be met, regardless of whatever level of output the firm is making and selling. We calculate the contribution a product makes towards the fixed costs by:

sales price
– variable costs
= contribution

Each 'contribution' goes towards paying the firm's fixed costs. When enough of these contributions have been made, the firm's fixed costs will be covered (paid): this is the break-even point.

If we use the information in Fig. 6.7, the selling price is £3.00 and the variable cost 50p per unit. The contribution is therefore:

£3.00 – 50p = £2.50

Each item sold contributes £2.50 towards the firm's fixed costs, which total £10 000. We can calculate the break-even point by **dividing the total fixed costs by the unit contribution**. If we do this, we see that 4000 is (as we have read from the chart) the firm's break-even point.

$$\frac{\textbf{total fixed costs}}{\textbf{unit contribution}} \quad = \quad \frac{\textbf{10 000}}{\textbf{2.50}} \quad = \textbf{4000}$$

> Check the chart, to see if the company is losing £2500 at an output of 3000 units.

We can also calculate the amount of profit or loss at each level of production/sales. For example, output and sales of 3000 produce a total contribution of £7500 (3000 x £2.50): since fixed costs are still £10 000, the company must be making a loss of £2500 here.

PROGRESS CHECK

1. State the difference between:
   (a) direct and indirect costs
   (b) fixed and variable costs
2. Define 'break-even point'. How is it calculated?

1. (a) Direct costs are directly linked to product lines; indirect are more general (overheads).
   (b) Fixed do not change with output; variable do.
2. Break-even point is that output where neither a profit nor a loss is being made. It can be calculated by dividing total fixed costs by unit contribution.

6.3 Forecasting and budgeting

LEARNING SUMMARY

After studying this section you should be able to understand:

● *the need for budgeting*
● *the importance of cash forecasting*

Budgeting

AQA A   AQA B
EDEXCEL
OCR A   OCR B
WJEC
NICCEA

Forecasting and budgeting help us to **plan ahead**. A firm's budget is a detailed forecast of future plans and action for the business, measured in money – in the same way that a household budget tries to plan a family's income and expenditure.

KEY POINT   A **budget is** a plan that is stated in financial terms.

The need for budgeting

A firm's management must do the following.

1. **Plan for the future**. Managers collect information that helps them plan in advance: they can then, at a later date, **compare the actual results with their planned results**.
2. **Set performance targets**. Managers must consult with, and delegate responsibility to, their own staff. All staff can be involved in preparing the budgets, which will motivate them as well as encouraging them to think ahead and to take on further responsibility.
3. **Take prompt action**. Comparing budgeted (planned) performance with actual performance will produce differences known as **variances**. These variances can be analysed, and acted upon by the managers concerned.

Budget preparation

A traditional manufacturing company prepares the budgets summarised in Fig. 6.8.

Budget	Content
sales	planned future sales; number and price of each product line sold
production	output of products; output each week
stock	how much raw material to buy, when, and where from
fixed assets	cost of, and where to buy, new fixed assets such as machinery
final accounts	the forecast profit and loss account, and forecast balance sheet
cash	planned cash inflows and outflows in the period, and when these should take place

Fig. 6.8 Budgets

This is known as integrating the budgets.

Preparing budgets can't take place in isolation. For example, the sales budget will be used to help calculate the advertising budget, and it will also be used when planning the production budget (what to make, and when).

> **KEY POINT**
> **Planning and budgeting help managers to control the firm through having to control their own departments.**

Cash budgeting and forecasting

AQA A   AQA B
EDEXCEL
OCR A   OCR B
WJEC
NICCEA

We know that all firms must have sufficient working capital (page 110), so they can meet their debts as these become due for payment. Lack of working capital could mean that:

- the firm can't pay its staff on time
- it cannot take advantage of cash discounts it has been offered for prompt payment
- it can't pay its creditors at all, which may lead to legal action by these creditors to recover their money, causing the firm to close down

Working capital and cash budgeting

We forecast the movement of cash by identifying:

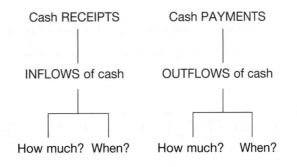

Fig. 6.9 Movement of cash

Companies that publish their accounts have to include a cash flow forecast to accompany their profit and loss account and balance sheet.

It is important to forecast, and to budget for, working capital and cash flows. By preparing forecasts of cash coming in and going out of the firm, the accountant will identify times of the year when there will be **shortfalls** of cash, so (for example) an overdraft can be arranged with the firm's bank. **Surpluses** of cash will also be shown, and these surpluses can be invested by the firm on a short-term basis.

Fig. 6.10 is the layout of a typical cash budget. It shows the planned future cash movements, so that managers can see the effects of their plans on the firm's cash flow.

CASH FLOW BUDGET	January £000	February £000	March £000
INFLOWS			
Sales	450	420	470
Other Income	50	30	40
TOTAL INFLOWS	500	450	510
OUTFLOWS			
Raw Materials	60	80	110
Wages	80	80	90
Selling Expenses	10	20	25
Rent and Rates	5	5	5
Light and Heat	5	5	5
Buying Assets		300	50
Other Outflows	25	10	30
TOTAL OUTFLOWS	185	500	315
NET CASH SURPLUS OR DEFICIT	315	(50)	195
BALANCE FROM LAST MONTH	25	340	290
CASH BALANCE TO CARRY FORWARD	340	290	485

Fig. 6.10 A cash budget

PROGRESS CHECK

1. What is a budget?
2. Why is it important to forecast future cash flows?

1. A plan expressed in money.
2. To ensure there that expected cash shortfalls can be covered, e.g. by overdrafts, and that any surpluses can be anticipated and acted upon (e.g. through short-term investment).

6.4 Financial accounting

LEARNING SUMMARY

After studying this section you should be able to understand:

- *why financial accounting is important*
- *what 'profitability' and 'liquidity' mean*
- *final accounts: the profit and loss account and the balance sheet*
- *what the published accounts of companies contain*

The purposes of financial accounting

AQA A   AQA B
EDEXCEL
OCR A   OCR B
WJEC
NICCEA

We have to collect information about the financial position of the firm so that **financial control** can take place. This is vital to all organisations, whether they exist to make a profit or to provide a service to the community.

The accountant is the person we associate with controlling the finances of a firm. He or she will **study the firm's various financial options**: for example, by calculating whether it is better financially to hire or buy a machine.

The accountant will then **recommend the best financial course of action** on the basis of these alternatives. In our above example, the accountant would present figures showing the costs of hiring and the costs of buying the machine (including buying for cash and buying on credit).

> **Financial accounting:**
> - obtains financial information
> - records financial information
> - analyses ficancial infromation
> - presents financial information

KEY POINT

Obtaining information

The accounts department of a firm gets its information from various sources. An example is when the sales department sends copies of its sales invoices to accounts, from which the quantity and value of the firm's sales can be calculated. Also, the firm's incoming mail will contain cheques from debtors that have to be banked, and statements from creditors that must be paid.

Recording information

Information is recorded in the firm's accounts: this is the **book-keeping** element of financial accounting. The collection of the firm's accounts is known as '**The Ledger**', these accounts often being grouped together in this way:

- the **sales ledger** contains customer accounts
- the **purchases** (or **bought**) **ledger** keeps the accounts of the firm's suppliers
- the **cash book** contains details of the firm's cash and bank accounts
- the **general ledger** is where all the other accounts are found

Analysing information

Once the details of the financial transactions are recorded, the accountant can analyse this information. This is often done by calculating **accounting ratios** (page 114), which highlight trends that can be discussed with managers. These managers may also be involved in 'advance planning' – being asked to produce **budgets** so the future performance of their departments can be planned and monitored.

Presenting information

The accountant has a key role as a **communicator** of information, presenting it to the rest of the management team. There are various groups of people who are interested in this financial information:

> Some of these groups are internal (directors, managers, employees) to the firm: the rest are external.

Fig. 6.11 The groups who are interested in financial information

Profitability and liquidity

AQA A   AQA B
EDEXCEL
OCR A   OCR B
WJEC
NICCEA

When studying a firm's financial performance, we check its profitability and liquidity. We know that not all organisations are set up with the aim of making a profit – many sports and social clubs, for example. However, even these non-profitmaking organisations must still 'account' for their financial performance.

Profitability

> Profit is both a reward for risk-taking and an internal source of funds for a business.

One reason for keeping accounts is to record the firm's **revenues** (income) and **expenses**, from which we can calculate its profit. We then compare the amount of this profit to other important figures, especially the value of sales made and the value of the capital invested in the firm. This gives a guide to its **profitability**.

> **KEY POINT**
>
> 'Profitability' and 'profit' are related but different: profitability assesses whether the profit figure is adequate by comparing it to sales and capital.

Liquidity

A firm's liquidity refers to its ability to meet its debts as they fall due. A firm will have both **current assets** (cash and 'near-cash' items such as its stock, and the money owed by its debtors) and **current liabilities** (its own short-term debts, such as the money it owes to its suppliers). Its **working capital** is the difference between its current assets and its current liabilities.

		£000	£000
Current assets			
	Stock		250
	Debtors		490
	Cash in Hand		10
			750
Current liabilities			
	Creditors	370	
	Bank Overdraft	30	
			400
Working capital			350

Fig. 6.12 A company's working capital

Why is the amount of working capital important? **It shows whether the firm is in a position to pay its debts.** If, for example, its current assets are £30 000 and its current liabilities are £20 000, the firm has enough cash and 'near-cash' to meet the £20 000 debts due shortly. If, however, these figures were £20 000 current assets and £30 000 current liabilities, it looks as though the firm might struggle to find enough money to pay its debts.

Final accounts

AQA A AQA B
EDEXCEL
OCR A OCR B
WJEC
NICCEA

At the end of each financial year a firm will produce a set of 'final accounts':

- its **profit and loss account** calculates net profit
- its **balance sheet** displays its assets and its liabilities

The trading account

Sales revenue is also known as turnover.

The profit and loss account contains a section – sometimes referred to as a separate account – showing the firm's trading (its buying and selling). The purpose of the trading account is to calculate **gross profit**: Fig. 6.13 shows that this is the difference between the sales revenue and the cost of these sales.

N. Merchant Trading account for year ending 31 December	£ (000)	£ (000)
Sales		400
Less cost of sales:		
Opening stock	55	
Purchases	290	
	345	
Closing stock	(45)	
		300
Gross profit		**100**

Fig. 6.13 The trading account

The profit and loss account

The purpose of this account is to calculate the firm's **net profit**: this is the balance that's left after all the expenses have been deducted from the gross profit. There will be various administration, and selling and distribution expenses: examples include rent and rates, light and heat, wages and salaries, and these two items:

1. **depreciation**, which is the cost of 'using up' the major assets of the business, e.g. through the wear and tear on furniture, vehicles and machinery
2. **bad debts**, the cost of selling on credit – when a debtor cannot pay the debt owed to the firm, the firm has to write the debtor off as an expense

N. Merchant Profit and loss account for year ending 31 December	£ (000)	£ (000)
Gross profit		100
Less expenses:		
Administration	32	
Selling and distribution	16	
Financial	12	
		60
Net profit		**40**

Fig. 6.14 The profit and loss account

The balance sheet

> Capital expenditure, by being shown in the balance sheet, does not affect the calculation of business profit.

The purpose of the balance sheet is to show us what the firm **owns** (assets), and what it **owes** (liabilities). Payment that the firm has made for its assets is called **capital expenditure**, and we see the result of this expenditure in the balance sheet in the form of assets.

Items in the balance sheet often appear under these headings.

N.Merchant Balance sheet as at 31 December	£ (000)	£ (000)	£ (000)
	Cost	Depreciation	Net
Fixed assets			
Land and buildings	100	—	100
Plant and equipment	24	6	18
Vehicles	5	3	2
	129	9	120
Current assets			
Stocks		45	
Debtors		25	
Bank and cash		20	
		90	
Current liabilities			
Creditors	20		
Accrued expenses	10		
		30	
Net current assets			60
Net assets			180
Capital			
Opening balance			140
Net profit for year			40
			180

Fig. 6.15 The balance sheet

- **Fixed assets**: these assets have a long life, and are not bought to re-sell.
- **Current assets**: these are assets that link closely with trading, and which are used directly to make a profit.
- **Current liabilities**: these are often shown as deductions from current assets, to give the working capital figure (also known as **net current assets**). Companies have two important current liabilities: **proposed dividends** are amounts they owe to their shareholders and will pay in the form of dividends, and **corporation tax** shows how much they owe to the government as tax on their profits.
- **Capital**: this shows us the value of the owners' investment.

Capital includes:
- **share capital** – this indicates the total value of the investment made by the various shareholders
- **reserves** – including undistributed profits that are being kept in the company to help it expand
- **loan capital** (e.g. debentures) – an important source of long-term finance for companies

> **KEY POINT**
> The profit and loss account shows the firm's financial performance; the balance sheet shows its financial position.

Published accounts

AQA A   AQA B
EDEXCEL
OCR A   OCR B
WJEC
NICCEA

Public limited companies must publish their final accounts. This allows interested groups, such as those shown in Fig. 6.11, to study the financial information.

The **Annual Report and Accounts** document published by a plc contains not only its final accounts, but also a lot of other information. This includes:

- a 'financial highlights' summary
- the Chairman's statement and a statement by the Chief Executive giving a broad outline of the company's achievements in the year
- a detailed financial or operating (trading) review
- the Directors' report on the company's performance
- the actual final accounts (profit and loss account, and balance sheet, plus a cash-flow statement), together with notes that explain these accounts
- the auditors' report confirming that the accounts are fair
- a summary of the last five years' financial performance

> **KEY POINT** Plcs have to disclose a lot of financial information by law.

Here are some extracts from published accounts that we can compare with the other examples of final accounts in this chapter.

Group profit and loss account for the 52 weeks to 1 April 2000

	2000 £m	1999 £m
Turnover (net of VAT)	16 271	16 433
Cost of sales	(15 201)	(15 116)
Gross profit	1 070	1 317
Expenses	(542)	(481)
Operating profit	528	836
Other profit	53	107
Profit before interest	581	943
Interest payable	(72)	(55)
Profit before tax	509	888
Tax	(162)	(292)
Profit after tax	347	596
Minority interests	2	2
Profit for the year	349	598
Dividends	(274)	(294)
Retained profit	75	304

Group balance sheets, 1 April 2000 and 3 April 1999

	2000 £m	1999 £m
Fixed assets	6 977	6 450
Current assets:		
stocks	986	843
debtors	320	249
investments	18	17
Sainsbury's Bank	1 718	1 766
bank and cash	533	725
	3 575	3 600
Current liabilities	(4 720)	(4 549)
Net current liabilities	(1 145)	(949)
Total assets less		
current liabilities	5 832	5 501
Long-term liabilities	(1 041)	(812)
Net assets	4 791	4 689
Capital and reserves:		
called-up share capital	481	480
other reserves	4 261	4 164
Minority interest	49	45
	4 791	4 689

Fig 6.16 Extracts from published accounts (Source: J Sainsbury plc Annual Report and Accounts 2000)

PROGRESS CHECK

1. What does the accounting function do with financial information?.
2. Explain the difference between profitability and liquidity.

2. Profitability measures profit against turnover/capital; liquidity assesses ability to pay debts as they become due for payment.

1. Obtain; record; analyse; present.

6.5 *Interpreting accounts*

After studying this section you should be able to understand:

● *profitability, liquidity and efficiency ratios*
● *why it is important to calculate ratios*

Areas for analysis

Part of the accountant's work is to analyse the financial performance of the firm. The accountant will analyse the firm's **profitability** (page 110) and **liquidity** (page 110), and also how efficiently it is using assets such as its stock. To do this, a series of **ratios** will be calculated.

Profitability ratios

Name	Calculation	Purpose
GROSS PROFIT MARGIN (%)	$\dfrac{\text{Gross Profit}}{\text{Turnover}} \times 100$	To show what percentage of turnover is represented by gross profit (how many pence out of every £1 sales is gross profit).

If this percentage is increasing, the firm will be receiving more gross profit for every £1 in sales. If this is falling, the firm's profit margin is smaller than before (e.g. it has cut its selling price, or its costs of sales are more expensive).

Name	Calculation	Purpose
NET PROFIT MARGIN (%)	$\dfrac{\text{Net Profit}}{\text{Turnover}} \times 100$	To show what percentage of turnover is represented by net profit.

An increase in this percentage means that the firm is making a higher net profit per £1 of sales than before. This may be due to a change in the gross profit percentage or perhaps the firm's expenses (as a percentage of sales) have fallen.

Name	Calculation	Purpose
RETURN ON CAPITAL EMPLOYED ('ROCE')	$\dfrac{\text{Net Profit}}{\text{Capital Employed}} \times 100$	To show how profitable the owners' investment is by calculating the percentage return.

This figure – how many pence net profit out of every £1 capital employed – can then be compared to the rate of return the owners would like to receive if they invested elsewhere. This indicates to them whether it is worthwhile continuing to invest in the business.

Liquidity ratios

Name	Calculation	Purpose
WORKING CAPITAL RATIO	Current Assets to Current Liabilities (as a ratio)	To check the ability of the business to pay its short-term debts.
LIQUID CAPITAL ('ACID TEST') RATIO	Current Assets less Stock, to Current Liabilities (as a ratio)	To see whether the business can meet its short-term debts without having to sell any stock.

Asset efficiency ratios

Name	Calculation	Purpose
RATE OF STOCK TURNOVER ('STOCKTURN')	Cost of Sales/Average Stock	To give the number of times per period that the average stock is sold.

> We calculate average stock by totalling the opening and closing stock figures, then dividing this total by 2.

If the stockturn is increasing, it's likely that the firm is holding lower average stocks than before and is operating more efficiently; and vice versa.

Name	Calculation	Purpose
DEBTORS' COLLECTION PERIOD	$\dfrac{\text{Debtors}}{\text{Turnover}} \times 365$	To show the length of time (number of days) on average that it takes debtors to pay their debts to the business.

Name	Calculation	Purpose
CREDITORS' COLLECTION PERIOD	$\dfrac{\text{Creditors}}{\text{Cost of Sales}} \times 365$	To show the length of time, in days, that the business takes to pay its creditors.

The debtors' collection period shows how efficient the firm is at collecting its debts: if the number of days is falling, it is being more efficient, and vice versa. With the creditors' collection period, any increase here means that the firm is taking a longer credit period, either because it's better at getting credit, or because it is facing problems in paying its creditors.

Using ratios

Study the following final accounts. We can use these figures to calculate some important ratios.

TRADING and PROFIT and LOSS ACCOUNTS
for the Year Ended 31 December

	£000	£000
Turnover		1000
less: Cost of Sales		
Opening Stock	40	
Purchases	620	
	660	
Closing Stock	60	
		600
Gross Profit		400
less: Expenses		
Rent and Rates	20	
Light and Heat	10	
Advertising	25	
Wages and Salaries	70	
Office Expenses	125	
Depreciation	45	
Bad Debts	5	
		300
Net Profit		100

BALANCE SHEET as at 31 December

	£000	£000	£000
FIXED ASSETS			
Premises			200
Machinery			60
Vehicles			40
			300
CURRENT ASSETS			
Closing Stock		60	
Debtors		100	
Cash at Bank		20	
		180	
CURRENT LIABILITIES			
Creditors	60		
Proposed Dividend	20		
Unpaid Corporation Tax	40	120	
NET CURRENT ASSETS			60
NET ASSETS			360
Financed by:			
SHARE CAPITAL			
200 000 £1 Ordinary Shares			200
RESERVES			
General Reserve		70	
Undistributed Profits		30	100
LOAN CAPITAL			
Debentures			60
			360

Fig. 6.17 Final accounts

Using the figures from these final accounts, the ratios are:

- **Gross profit margin.** $\dfrac{400}{1000} \times 100 = 40\%$

Gross profit is 40p for every £1 of sales (therefore the remaining 60p in the pound represents the firm's cost of sales).

- **Net profit margin.** $\dfrac{100}{1000} \times 100 = 10\%$

Every £1 of sales gives 10p net profit: the difference between the 40p gross profit and 10p net profit represents the expenses (30p in every £1 of sales).

- **Return on capital employed.** $\dfrac{100}{300} \times 100 = 33.3\%$

Every £1 of capital employed (we've used the capital invested plus reserves figure) in the business earns about 33p profit for the shareholders.

- **Working capital ratio.** 180 : 120 = 3 : 2 (1½ : 1) current assets to current liabilities. The firm has £1.50 cash or 'near cash' with which to pay every £1 of its short-term debts.

The other name for the liquid assets ratio is the 'Acid test'.

- **Liquid assets ratio.** (180 – 60 stock =) 120 : 120, or 1 : 1 liquid assets to current liabilities. The firm, without selling any stock, can meet its short-term debts from its liquid assets.

- **Rate of stock turnover.** $\dfrac{600}{50} = 12$ times a year.

The firm takes a month, on average, to 'turn over' (buy and sell) its stock.

- **Debtors' collection period.** $\dfrac{100}{1000} \times 365 = 36.5$ days

Debtors take, on average, just over five weeks to pay their debts owed to the firm.

- **Creditors' collection period.** $\dfrac{60}{600} \times 365 = 36.5$ days

The firm also takes, on average, 36.5 days' credit from its suppliers.

> **KEY POINT**
>
> Ratios are no use on their own: we must compare this year's ratios for a firm to (a) previous ones for this firm to see trends, and (b) those of its competitors to check competitiveness.

PROGRESS CHECK

1. Name:
   - **(a) two** profitability ratios
   - **(b) two** liquidity ratios
   - **(c) two** efficiency ratios

1. (a) Net profit margin, ROCE
(b) Current ratio, liquid ratio
(c) Stockturn, debtor days

Sample GCSE questions

1. Extracts from *Happy Ideas Ltd's* financial statements for 1997 and 1996 are given below.

	1997 £	1996 £
Turnover	2 121 920	2 074 621
Expenses	1 878 924	2 018 285
Fixed Assets	275 833	131 062
Current Assets	902 440	822 969
Current Liabilities	366 413	344 912
Capital & Reserves	811 860	609 119

(Source: Merrythought Ltd.)

(a) **(i)** Give another name for turnover. **(1)**

Another name is Gross Profit

This is wrong: 'turnover' is the other name for sales.

(ii) List THREE expenses. **(3)**

Rent; machinery; wages.

Two are correct but 'machinery' is a fixed asset, not an expense.

(iii) Identify which item in the financial statements above would show debtors. **(1)**

Current assets

(iv) Identify which item in the financial statements above would show creditors. **(1)**

Current liabilities

Both are correct.

Sample GCSE questions

(b) **(i)** Using the information above, calculate the working capital for 1997. (Show your working.) **(2)**

Current assets £902 440 - current liabilities
£366 413 = £536 027

A good answer. Workings are shown (very important in figure-work); you can still get marks for a wrong answer if you show you know how to do the calculation correctly.

(ii) What problems would the directors of *Happy Ideas Ltd* face if the company became short of working capital? **(4)**

The main problem the directors would face is that they wouldn't be able pay debts. This means that Happy Ideas Ltd wouldn't be able to pay people like its employees, or its suppliers. If this happens, they won't get materials and won't be able to make and sell their products.

A good answer, though draw a conclusion: the directors may face going out of business if they don't meet debts.

(c) **(i)** Compare the Fixed Assets and the Capital & Reserves for the two years. **(4)**

The figures show that both the Fixed Assets and the Capital & Reserves have increased.

This is correct, but the amount of the increase should be calculated: £144 771 and £202 741 respectively.

(ii) Suggest possible reasons for changes in the Fixed Assets and the Capital & Reserves. **(4**

With Fixed Assets, more could have been bought because the company is expanding. Capital & Reserves increase by either putting more capital in, or keeping some of the profits as reserves.

Again, this is a good answer, but it would be improved by giving examples of fixed assets that might have been bought (machinery, equipment), and by stating who has put more capital in (shareholders).

Edexcel Paper 1, 2000

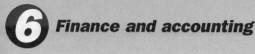

Exam practice questions

1. Jeff Jones had been made redundant from a multinational textile producer in mid Wales. He decided to use his redundancy money to set up his own business and work from home. Jeff had collected old postcards for many years and he decided to frame enlarged copies of his postcards to sell at craft and antique fairs. He intends to pay himself a wage of £100 at each fair. Each framed picture sells for £10.

His costs at each fair are:

Wages	£100
Rent for hiring a stall	£30
Travel costs to and from fairs	£20
Production costs per frame	£5

(a) What is meant by the term *break-even*? **(1)**

(b) On the graph below draw and label a break-even chart.

Cost/revenue (£)

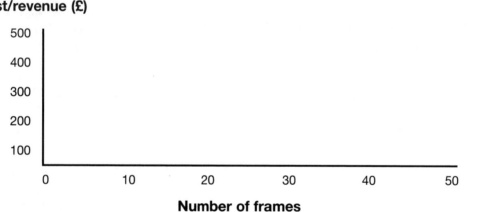

Number of frames

(c) Using the graph state the number of frames Jeff would need to break even at each fair. **(1)**

(d) On average Jeff is able to sell 50 frames per fair. Using the graph calculate the amount of profit he makes at each fair. **(1)**

(e) Jeff's total income consists of the wages he pays himself plus the profits from each fair. He would like his total income to be at least £15 000 per year. Calculate the number of fairs he would need to attend in a year to achieve this income. **(2)**

(f) Jeff receives a substantial order from a chain of shops. He realises that an order of this size will create problems. Identify the major business problems that this new order is likely to present and assess how these problems can be overcome. **(8)**

WJEC Specimen Paper 2

7 Marketing

The following topics are included in this chapter:

- Market and products
- Market research
- The product
- Pricing decisions
- Promotion
- Place

7.1 Markets and products

LEARNING SUMMARY

After studying this section you should be able to understand:

- **the meaning of the term 'market'**
- **consumer and industrial markets**
- **the importance of the 'four Ps'**
- **how markets can be segmented**

Markets

AQA A AQA B
EDEXCEL
OCR A OCR B
WJEC
NICCEA

> The market system relies on the price mechanism, market prices being influenced by supply and demand.

What is a market? A market is a place where **buyers and sellers are in contact** with each other. It exists where goods and services are bought and sold. Many people think of 'the market' as a particular **place**: for example, in a town or village, a group of market stalls selling a range of items. With other products or services, a **specialist** market may exist, such as a stock exchange concentrating on buying and selling company stocks and shares. We are also part of the **labour** market, selling our qualifications and expertise to meet employers' needs for qualified staff. We can therefore think of 'the market' as being local, national or international, such as the labour market, or the market for cars or digital televisions.

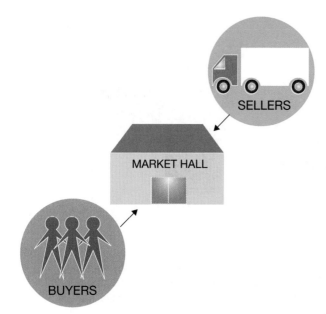
Fig. 7.1 Buyers and sellers in contact

Types of market

We know that many different types of 'market' exist. We normally put them under two headings.

1. **Consumer markets** supply goods and services to consumers like us. These consist of:

- **single-use** consumer goods, such as food or domestic power
- **consumer durables**, e.g. DVD players, fridge-freezers and TVs
- **consumer services**, such as hairdressers or dentists

2. **Industrial** (or **commercial**) **markets** supply the goods and services needed by firms.

Examples include:
- **capital goods** (major items, 'assets' such as new machines and equipment)
- **industrial services**, e.g. office cleaning, stationery printing, transport services

 A company such as *The Sock Shop* illustrates how a firm can concentrate successfully on a niche market.

We can also analyse markets in terms of their **size**. A consumer market may be a '**mass market**': for example, consumer durables, and some foodstuffs. Within these markets we may also find **niche** markets: for example, the market for food contains niche markets as a result of the different cultural or religious rules that are associated with certain types of food.

> **KEY POINT**
> Customers' needs and wants change all the time, and markets respond to these changes.

The marketing department and the marketing mix

'The market' to a firm consists of its **actual and potential customers**, those people and/or organisations that demand the firm's products.

'Marketing' has been defined (by the Chartered Institute of Marketing) as '**The anticipation, identification and fulfilment of a consumer need – at a profit**'. What does this definition tell us? The words 'anticipation' and 'identification' refer to the role of **market research**, carried out by the firm's marketing department. It is the role of this department to research into the market, to provide information on market conditions so the firm can:

The 'four Ps' are closely linked, and should not be thought of as separate from each other.

- design and supply **products** that are demanded by the market
- **place** the products in the market
- support products with suitable **promotion**
- sell products at an appropriate **price**

By doing so, consumer needs are **fulfilled** (our definition mentions 'fulfilment') and the firm should make a **profit**.

Fig. 7.2 The marketing mix

> **KEY POINT**
> An efficient and appropriate 'mix' of the four Ps – product, price, place and promotion – should mean that the firm will survive and make a profit for its owners.

Markets and segmentation

AQA A AQA B
EDEXCEL
OCR A OCR B
WJEC
NICCEA

The market for a product can often be broken down into different **segments** (sections). For example, the car market in the UK consists of a number of segments: Fig. 7.3 illustrates how we might segment this market.

FAMILY CAR
Medium or large size
Plenty of luggage space
Interior comfort

COMPANY CAR
Easy to service
Easy to sell after new repalcement cars are bought

SECOND CAR
Small
Economical to run
Inexpensive to buy

Fig. 7.3 Market segments

Segmenting the market

> Cars such as the Ford Ka and other small hatchbacks may be targeted at the 'second car' market. Other cars, e.g. Rolls Royce, will be targeted at the 'luxury car' segment.

Our example above shows us that car (and other) firms may decide to produce **particular models for particular segments**. By doing so, the firm can plan its advertising campaign to appeal to customers in these segments.

Each market segment will have its own unique requirements, and will therefore need a different 'mix' of marketing resources – because market segments (and markets in general) vary in their make-up. Consumers in these markets and segments will differ in the following ways.

1. **Age**. This is an important influence on product features, such as the way youth fashion influences the style of clothes that a clothing manufacturer may decide to market.

> The trend towards smaller family units and greater demand for single-person accommodation has, for example, influenced house design and construction.

2. **Population**. The overall size and geographical distribution of the population is important when marketing products, e.g. for decisions on how to transport, how to advertise and where to store the firm's products.

3. **Groupings**. Firms will be interested in the various groups that make up their markets and market segments. Different religious and cultural groupings in the population have their own specialist demand for items such as foodstuffs, and the number and size of family groups is important to those companies marketing products such as baby clothes and toys.

4. **Income**. The size of **disposable** income will help decide, for example, the quality of the products marketed, and how many models – 'standard', 'super' etc. – a firm decides to make and market.

> **KEY POINT**
> Targeting products at distinct market segments allows firms to focus their 'four Ps' (especially promotion) on these segments.

PROGRESS CHECK

1. Give **three** further examples of:
   (a) consumer markets
   (b) industrial markets
2. State **four** ways in which a market may be segmented.

2. Age; population; groupings within the population; disposable income.
(b) Industrial: market for computers, packaging materials, office desks.
1. (a) Consumer: market for crockery, wallpaper, garden furniture.

7.2 Market research

 **LEARNING SUMMARY**

After studying this section you should be able to understand:

* *the role of market research*
* *primary and secondary types of market research*

The role of market research

AQA A · AQA B · EDEXCEL · OCR A · OCR B · WJEC · NICCEA

 Market research information will also be used in new product development and for production decisions.

Market research provides the firm's marketing department with information about the elements of the marketing mix. What will the marketing department research into? Factors such as:

* the market itself
* the likely demand for the products
* the variety of models demanded by the consumers
* the price(s) to charge
* how the product should be advertised and distributed

The management of a firm involved in market research has the choice of using its own marketing department, or employing a **specialist market research organisation**.

KEY POINT

Marketing, through seeking to identify consumer wants and predict their future wants, uses market research to collect and analyse information about the marketplace.

Methods of market research

AQA A · AQA B · EDEXCEL · OCR A · OCR B · WJEC · NICCEA

There are two main methods of market research: **primary** research and **secondary** research.

Primary
* also known as **field** research
* obtains **new** information

Secondary
* also known as **desk** research
* uses **existing** sources of information

Primary (field) research

There are various methods of field research available to a firm. Each method involves using one or more of the following investigation techniques.

* **Questionnaires** – designed specifically for the task, and completed by holding interviews with potential consumers either face-to-face 'in the street', over the telephone, or through the post.
* **Test marketing** – this is where a potential new product is marketed in one area of the country only, and the reactions to it are studied to see whether it should be launched nationally or abandoned.
* **Consumer panels** – people are selected to join a panel, are then given the product and asked to provide detailed comments on it.

The major advantage that primary research has over secondary is that **it is carried out specifically for the product in question**. Desk (or secondary) research uses information collected for other purposes, and so won't be fully relevant to the firm's own product.

Secondary (desk) research

A company planning to use desk research may find there are a number of sources to use.

Detailed investigation of competitor products is often used in 'hi-tec' industries, such as computer and games hardware/software.

- **Its own sales statistics** – these can identify sales trends, consumer suggestions for product changes, or requests for new models.
- **Competitors' products** – products already on the market can be investigated, to discover popular/unpopular features, in order to help the firm design a better product.
- **Government and other statistics** – figures showing trends in spending patterns, population movement and growth and so on are available from the EU and UK governments, as well as being found in 'broadsheet' papers such as *The Guardian*, *The Financial Times* and *The Independent*.

Here's an example of secondary statistics that the retailers featuring in them could use.

Percentage share of grocery market, 1988 and 1998

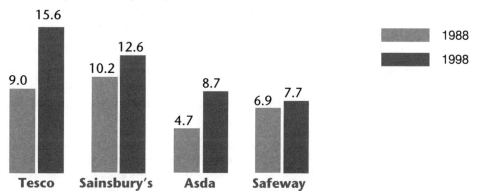

Fig. 7.4 Secondary statistics: the 'big four' retailers in the UK, 1988–1998

Secondary research has two main advantages over primary: it is **less expensive**, and it is **quicker to obtain** because the information is already available.

> **KEY POINT**
> The type and amount of market research carried out by a firm is influenced by the firm's size and its resources.

PROGRESS CHECK

1. What is the main advantage that field research has over desk research?

1. The information collected relates exclusively to the product being researched.

7.3 The product

After studying this section you should be able to understand:

- *the nature of the 'product mix'*
- *a common way to analyse the product mix*
- *stages in the product life-cycle*
- *the nature of product differentiation*

The product mix

Many firms make and sell a variety of products. The range of products sold is known as the **product mix**.

Choosing the mix

The firm's choice of product mix is influenced by answering these two questions.

1. Do we want to concentrate on a single segment of the market, or sell products in most or all segments? For example, the major car manufacturers produce different models for different segments; and some holiday companies concentrate on certain segments only (e.g. 'Club 18–30', or Saga holidays for the over-50s).
2. How many products will we make and sell? Influences here include the strength and actions of the competition, and the profitability of the products being made.

> **This diversified approach helps firms if one of their products fails in its market.**

> **KEY POINT**
> Products in the mix should be **compatible**: they should normally complement (support) each other, not compete with each other.

Analysing the mix

A popular way used to analyse a firm's product mix is to use the **Boston Consulting Group's matrix** (grid). It divides products into four categories, according to their market share and the nature of the market.

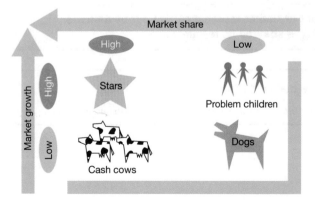

Fig. 7.5 The 'Boston box'

- **Stars**. These are potentially very profitable products for the firm, but they need large investment to turn them into 'cash cows'.
- **Problem children**. As their name suggests, they are a problem in terms of what is best to do with them – they may become stars with heavy investment, but are just as likely to turn into dogs.
- **Cash cows**. These are the firm's main products in terms of profitability and sales: often heavily promoted, they provide revenue for the firm to support its other products and new product development.

● **Dogs.** These are the more unprofitable, or even loss-making, products, which the firm normally gets rid of (unless they are being held for other reasons, e.g. to stop competitors getting into the market).

The product life-cycle

AQA A · AQA B
EDEXCEL
OCR A · OCR B
WJEC
NICCEA

> New technology, new inventions and changes in fashion are the main influences on the life of products.

Almost all products have a **finite** – limited – life, both from the consumer's viewpoint and also as far as the producer is concerned. As an example, a particular car model may last five or ten – or, in the case of the Mini, about 40 – years before it is phased out and replaced by a completely new model.

Some products may survive because they now sell in different segments of their original markets. For example, fountain pens – far less important nowadays in the popular pen market as a result of competing forms such as the 'biro' and roller-ball pens – compete successfully in the 'quality pen' market, and smaller colour TVs are increasingly sold in the 'second TV' market segment rather than as the main household television.

The life-cycle

Products therefore have a life-cycle. Although different products will be sold over different lengths of time, their life-cycles have certain elements in common, shown by Fig. 7.6.

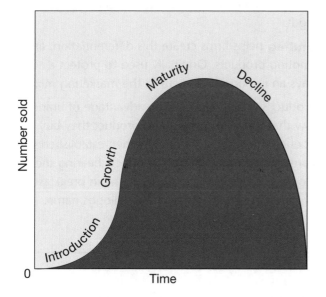

Fig. 7.6 Stages of the product life-cycle

● Following its development (normally following successful market research), which can take a long time, the product is introduced onto the market. This **Introduction** stage will be supported by heavy advertising and 'below-the-line' promotion (page 135). Initial sales will be low until consumers get to know of, and buy, the product. At this point, the costs of production – which often include huge development costs – are much higher than the revenue from sales.

● The **Growth** stage occurs as more and more consumers buy the product. It establishes a **brand loyalty** amongst its users, who will deliberately choose this product rather than a competing brand. Sales rise, and the product starts to become profitable as the sales revenue pays off the earlier development costs.

● At the **Maturity** stage, the product has reached its peak of sales. It is now fully established in the market, and at its most profitable for the company. It may have reached **market saturation**, and the firm's competitors may have brought out new competing, or modified their existing, products.

● The actions of competitors, changes in taste or fashion or in technology, or other influences all bring the product to the stage of **Decline**. Sales fall as its market share and influence reduces, and eventually the firm stops making and selling it.

> We may see a falling demand for VHS recorders due to DVD, and check old films and TV repeats to note changes in taste and fashion.

Extending the product's life

The length of the product's life-cycle can often be extended by **changing** it in some way. A popular method is relaunching a product as a 'new, improved' model. This is often linked to

- changes in **packaging**
- an **advertising campaign**
- **sales promotion** (e.g., the 'free gift' approach)

These steps are taken by a company in order to keep a product on the market for a longer period.

Other methods used to extend product life are to **adapt the product for a new market** (e.g. chocolate bars being made in ice cream format), and to **change the product's image** so that it appeals to a wider market (e.g. four-wheel drive, 'off road' vehicles being marketed for leisure).

 KEY POINT Firms usually find it less expensive and safer to extend the life of a well-known and popular product, rather than to gamble on producing a new one.

Product differentiation

The USP – Unique Selling Point – of products is used by firms when marketing them, e.g. Polo, 'the mint with the hole'.

Firms deliberately use different colours, shapes and sizes to differentiate and promote their products.

Firms need to be aware of how consumers see their products. A firm would, ideally, like its product to be regarded as **unique**, though it normally has to settle for the product being seen as different from that of its competitors. This **differentiation** allows the firm to concentrate on certain aspects of its product, e.g. when advertising it.

Product **packaging** and **branding** helps firms create this differentiation, and are also important when promoting products. Originally used to protect a product, packaging is nowadays an important element in the marketing mix.

The packaging displays the product's **brand name**. The advantage of branding to consumers is that they know that the next same-brand product they buy will be almost identical to the last one. The company's name, when established with one brand, may encourage consumers to buy different products bearing the same name: for example, Kelloggs is regarded as a quality name in breakfast cereals, so consumers may try different cereals carrying the Kelloggs name.

KEY POINT Product branding helps establish customer loyalty, and leads to repeat purchases.

 PROGRESS CHECK

1. Explain the difference between product mix and product differentiation.
2. Name
   (a) the **four** stages in the life-cycle of a product
   (b) the **four** elements of the 'Boston box'

1. Product mix indicates the range of products; product differentiation focuses on how firms create differences between their products and those of their competitors.
2. (a) Introduction; growth; maturity; decline.
   (b) Stars; cash cows; problem children; dogs.

7.4 Pricing decisions

LEARNING SUMMARY

After studying this section you should be able to understand:
- *the main internal and external influences on price*
- *high-price, low-price and other strategies used to price products*

Influences on the price

AQA A   AQA B
EDEXCEL
OCR A   OCR B
WJEC
NICCEA

Mark-up is an amount or percentage added to cost; margin is where profit is shown as an amount or percentage of the selling price.

Price is one of the four Ps in the marketing mix. The price that a firm decides to charge for its product will be influenced by internal **cost-based** and external **market-based** factors.

- With **internal** factors, costs of production are the main influence.
- With **external** factors, competitors' prices and the position of the firm in the market (its **market share** and whether it is **market dominant**) are important.

The firm's costs will influence the pricing formula that it uses to set a selling price. **Cost-plus pricing** (also known as **full-cost** pricing) may be used: here, the firm adds a profit **mark-up** onto its unit cost of production. If unit cost is, for example, £2.00, a mark-up of 50 % would give the firm a selling price of £3.00 (and a profit margin of £1.00). Cost-plus pricing has two main drawbacks: it is not easy to work out accurately the unit cost of production for products, and it ignores competitors' prices and products.

The use of **break-even analysis** (page 103) and **marginal costing** techniques (page 105) are also cost-based approaches that can be used when deciding on a price to charge: this is known as **contribution** pricing.

KEY POINT

Marketers prefer to concentrate on external (market) factors, whereas production managers are more influenced by the costs of production and the ease of making the product.

Pricing strategies

AQA A   AQA B
EDEXCEL
OCR A   OCR B
WJEC
NICCEA

The firm's management can use various pricing strategies for the firm's products.

High-price strategies

- With a **skimming** strategy, a firm launches a new and unique product, and decides to charge a high price to 'cream' the market (it is also known as **creaming** pricing). Some people will buy the product at this high price because of its 'status symbol' appeal. As this appeal dies down and competitors – attracted by the high profit margins – start selling their products, the firm reduces its prices.
- A **maximising** strategy may be used: where there is great demand for a product or service with a short life-cycle, the manufacturer will try to maximise profits by charging high prices.

- **Premium** pricing is used when a firm regards its product as the best in the market: as a result, it believes consumers will be prepared to pay for the high quality and the prestige (it is also known as **prestige** pricing) that comes from owning the product.

Low-price strategies

- Using a **penetration** policy, a low price is set so the firm can obtain a large market share. Prices may be increased later, to earn higher profits.

- A **capturing** strategy may be used if a company is making a range of products that are linked in some way. If, for example, the company is producing items of 'hardware' (equipment) and also making the software used by this equipment, it may sell the equipment at a low price and rely on charging high prices for the software.
- Firms may use the **loss leader** approach, selling a product at below cost price (or with a really low profit margin) in order to attract new consumers and increase its market share.

Other strategies

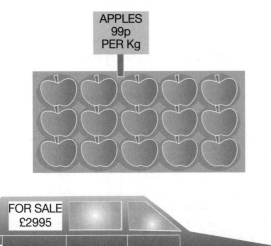

Fig. 7.7 'Odd' and 'psychological' pricing

These include the following:

1. **Odd pricing**. Prices end in odd numbers, e.g. 99p, £1.95.
2. **Psychological pricing**. This makes the item look cheaper by pricing it just below a 'round figure', e.g. £9.95 rather than £10, £2995 not £3000.
3. **Discrimination pricing**. This sets different prices in the different market segments. A good example comes from our public transport, where 'off-peak' fares are cheaper at set times of the day or week, and certain groups (e.g. students, senior citizens) can travel the same routes more cheaply than other users.
4. **Market pricing**. A '**price taker**' sets product prices at or near the current market rate, in order to avoid a price war.

> **KEY POINT**
> Firms may use a combination of these approaches to pricing, e.g. using psychological pricing as part of its penetration pricing policy.

> **PROGRESS CHECK**
> 1. What is the main internal influence on a firm's price?
> 2. State **two** high-price and **two** low-price strategies used by companies.
>
> 2. Skimming; premium. Penetration; capturing.
> 1. The full cost of making the product.

7.5 Promotion

LEARNING SUMMARY

After studying this section you should be able to understand:

● *the main methods of promotion*
● *the difference between 'persuasive' and 'informative' methods*
● *the role of advertising*
● *the other promotional methods – sales promotion, direct marketing, personal selling and public relations*

The main methods of promotion

AQA A   AQA B
EDEXCEL
OCR A   OCR B
WJEC
NICCEA

This 'competitive promotion' is often seen where products are substitutes for one another, e.g. butter and margarine, different types of lawn mowers.

Why firms promote

Firms promote their products for a number of reasons.

1. To **introduce new products onto the market**. Methods such as advertising can reach a wide audience who would otherwise not know about the product.
2. To **increase sales of existing products**, e.g. by promoting the product in a new market or segment.
3. To **compete with others**.
4. To **co-operate** with others (e.g. where a washing powder manufacturer teams up with a washing machine company).
5. To **improve company image**, e.g., the advertising of some multinational companies may concentrate on name and image rather than on products.

The four methods

Promotion uses four main methods: advertising, direct marketing, personal selling, and sales promotion. Sometimes a fifth – public relations – is included.

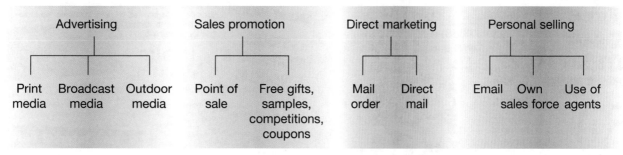

Advertising
 Print media   Broadcast media   Outdoor media

Sales promotion
 Point of sale   Free gifts, samples, competitions, coupons

Direct marketing
 Mail order   Direct mail

Personal selling
 Email   Own sales force   Use of agents

Fig. 7.8 The four main methods of promotion

1. **Advertising** is when a sponsor pays for the non-personal presentation of a message:

● advertising has a **sponsor**, someone – normally the manufacturer – who pays for the product to be advertised
● it is **paid for**, which distinguishes it from publicity (this is not paid for by the sponsor)
● it is **non-personal**, in other words it is directed at a mass audience rather than a particular individual (this distinguishes it from personal selling)

2. **Sales promotion** 'pushes' a product through activities such as displays, exhibitions, demonstrations and shows, and by offering incentives such as free samples and price reductions.
3. **Direct marketing** involves selling the firm's product by approaching consumers direct, rather than selling through retailers or dealers.
4. **Personal selling** provides the special individual information and contact, which advertising (being impersonal) can't.

> **KEY POINT**
> Branding **and product differentiation are important when it comes to** promoting a product.

Persuasive and informative approaches

Persuasive promotion

The objective of persuasive advertising and promotion is to **convince consumers that they need the product** being sold and, in particular, that they need **the firm's brand** of the product. Persuasive promotion is strongly supported by the use of branding, packaging and other forms of product differentiation.

Informative promotion

> One of the most commonly found types of informative advertisement is the job advert in the paper.

Here, the emphasis of the advertisement or other form of promotion is on giving full details (e.g. technical information) about the product. Informative advertising and promotion is often used by public service providers, for example in Yellow Pages or by the Government telling people about the harmful effects of smoking (although there is an element of persuasion with this last example).

Fig. 7.9 'Persuasive' and 'informative' advertising

> **KEY POINT**
> Although we often treat these forms as distinct, most advertising and promotion campaigns inform and try to persuade, and therefore contain elements of both.

Advertising

AQA A   AQA B
EDEXCEL
OCR A   OCR B
WJEC
NICCEA

> Advertising is known as 'above the line' promotion; the other promotional methods are called 'below the line'.

Advertising media

The **message** may be persuasive, informative or both. The **medium** is the method used to communicate this message.

- **Print-based media.** The advantages of advertising in papers and magazines rather than on TV and radio are that the advert is **permanent** (it can be cut out and kept or used in some way), and it can often give the reader much **more information**, although it will **lack impact** – it misses out on the sound and movement we have with the 'broadcast' type of advert.

  1. We can group **daily** and **Sunday** newspapers into the 'qualities' or 'broadsheets' such as *The Observer, The Times, The Guardian* and *The Independent,* and the 'tabloids' such as *The Mirror* and *The Sun*. All rely on advertising to make them profitable: the tabloids, due to their higher readership figures, tend to be more expensive for advertisers.

  2. **Regional** and **local** papers are also important media for getting messages across to large numbers of people, and are widely used by sellers with a local – rather than a national – demand and market.

  3. **Periodicals** and **specialist magazines** are often 'interest-based', such as the magazines that cater for particular sports and hobbies: advertisers can therefore **target** their adverts at an interested audience.

  4. **Free newspapers** ('free-sheets') rely on advertising for their survival: the advertising tends to be more informative, usually from local product/service businesses such as plumbers, garden centres and garages.

> We also find trade periodicals devoted to particular occupations or trades.

- **Broadcast media.**

  1. Large firms selling to a mass market may use **commercial TV**, which can be very persuasive and powerful, reaching (literally) millions of people. The adverts are expensive to broadcast, especially at the 'peak viewing' times that have large audiences. The advert has the advantage of **colour**, **sound** and **movement**, and may be tailored to particular groups and situations (e.g. children's toys adverts at Christmas).

  2. **Commercial radio** (both local and national) is much less expensive for advertisers because it reaches fewer people, although costs also vary according to the time the advert is broadcast. For example, it is more expensive during peak travel time when many people are listening in their cars.

  3. The **cinema** may also be used, with advertisers aiming their adverts at certain age groups.

> TV and radio advertising continues to grow as more and more cable/satellite TV channels and local radio stations are established.

- **Outdoor media.**

  1. **Posters** are widely used by many firms selling mass-appeal products. The position of large, permanent poster sites determines how much the poster will cost the firm to display. Posters are also a valuable medium for advertising local events.

  2. **Illuminated signs** are often used in city and town centres to draw attention to products or locations.

Influences on the advertisement

An advert's content, style and medium will be influenced by these factors.

> In 2000, this 10 cm space on the racing driver Michael Schumacher's baseball cap cost the German firm DVAG more than £5 million to place its logo on!

1. The size of the **advertising budget** will determine which media the company can afford for its campaign. When calculating 'media cost', the marketers must include not only the cost of using the various media, but also the expense involved in creating the advert.

> Television adverts in particular are very expensive to write and to film.

2. The **target group**. If this is a national one, then a national form of advertising will probably be chosen. The target audience may be special-interest, in which case a specialist magazine could be an appropriate medium. When the advert is to be informative in style, perhaps asking the audience to respond in some way, press advertising is likely to be used.

3. The **nature of the product**. Industrial-market products are often advertised in trade magazines, using an informative approach; consumer-oriented products often use the more persuasive techniques, and mass media such as television.

4. The position of the product in its **life-cycle**. Advertising tends to be more informative in the early days of the product's life, and increasingly persuasive as the product reaches maturity and decline.

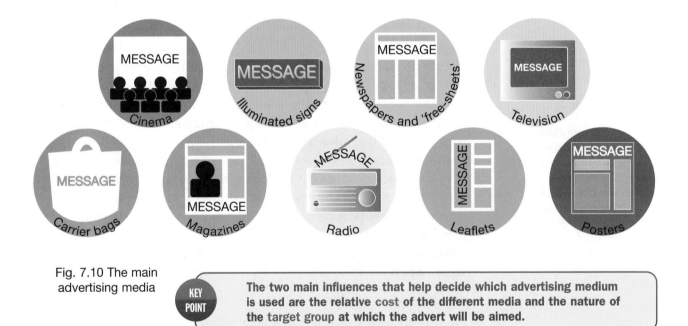

Fig. 7.10 The main advertising media

> **KEY POINT**
>
> The two main influences that help decide which advertising medium is used are the relative cost of the different media and the nature of the target group at which the advert will be aimed.

The advertising agency

Designing a professional advert can be a specialist activity, and so many firms employ advertising agencies for large-scale national advertising. These agencies may also provide a range of marketing expertise for interested firms: as well as carrying out advertising, the agency may undertake other work, such as carrying out market research on behalf of the firm.

The agency's advertising work consists of **selecting the medium** to be used, **writing** the advert, **designing** its overall appearance and style, and **arranging** its display or broadcast. It may also obtain **feedback** for the firm on the advert's success.

Arguments for and against advertising

1. Advertising provides **information** to consumers, who may not otherwise discover the product. This helps increase consumers' standard of living.
2. It **increases sales**, which leads to higher production and possibly more jobs, and also economies of scale leading to cheaper prices for consumers.
3. **Competition** is encouraged through advertising, which should again lead to lower prices.
4. **TV and newspapers are subsidised** through their advertising revenue.
5. **Employment** is created in the advertising industry.

BUT

1. **Higher prices** may occur if advertising is unsuccessful, because increased sales revenue won't cover advertising costs.
2. It can lead to **exploitation:**

- tempting people to buy what they don't need or can't afford
- encouraging them to buy products that may be harmful (e.g. alcohol) but which are sold using a tempting, advertising-created image
- tempting consumers to want more and more material possessions, with its appeal being emotional rather than rational

Other methods of promotion

AQA A   AQA B
EDEXCEL
OCR A   OCR B
WJEC
NICCEA

Sales promotion

This 'below-the-line' form of promotion allows sellers to promote their products by directly encouraging people to buy. **Point-of-sale (POS)**, also known as **merchandising**, is a popular sales promotion technique that **promotes the product where it is sold**. Point-of-sale displays, such as 'dump bins' or posters, are placed in good selling positions (e.g. by the till or at eye level). POS is often used with low-priced goods such as chocolate, because it encourages **impulse buying**.

After-sales service, like POS promotion, is an increasingly important form of promotion. Consumers may be tempted to buy products – particularly expensive, or technologically advanced ones – if the after-sales service is clearly linked with the product at the point or time of sale. A firm's **guarantee** relating to after-sale use of the product is often used as a sales promotion technique.

> A good example was when those car manufacturers who offered a three-year warranty on their new cars, compared with others only offering a one-year warranty, publicised this difference.

Sponsorship is sometimes used by firms to promote their image and products. For example, tobacco sponsorship has been used widely in some sports (such as Formula 1 motor racing), partly because tobacco cannot be advertised on television.

> Cruft's (dog products) and the Motor Show are examples of trade exhibitions.

Trade exhibitions are used to promote the sales of both consumer and industrial goods, and bring large numbers of sellers and buyers together.

These are the main sales promotion techniques that are directly linked to the product:

1. **free samples**, which have the advantage that potential customers actually try the product
2. **price reductions**, which encourage consumers to buy the product at, say, 10p off
3. **premium offers** where customers are offered free gifts (e.g. in breakfast cereal packets), send-away gifts (labels or tokens are collected and sent away), or low-priced purchase of goods (once sufficient labels have been collected and sent off)
4. **competitions** that encourage people to buy the product if there is a chance to win a cash or other prize

> A variation on price reduction is to give a coupon that offers a discount off the next purchase.

Fig. 7.11 Forms of sales promotion

> **KEY POINT**
> It can be easy to measure the effectiveness of sales promotions, e.g. by operating them in one area and not another, and then comparing sales.

Direct marketing

The methods we call 'direct marketing' all involve **direct approaches to the customer**. There are several forms of direct marketing, including:

- **mail order** catalogues, from which customers select and place their orders
- **direct mail**, for example leaflets asking for a customer response (e.g. a tear-off slip), and 'junk mail' sent directly through the post
- **email**, an increasingly popular electronic form of direct mail

> **KEY POINT**
> Direct marketing can be used selectively, and is often used to support other forms of promotion.

Personal selling

We know that advertising is impersonal, being directed at a mass audience. The use of personal selling allows the firm's message to be personally **tailored to the individual buyer**. Sales staff will have the responsibility of liaising with the customer: they will **deliver** the product; they can provide **demonstrations** and **technical information**; and they can also **pass on sales promotion materials** such as free samples or product leaflets, as well as **handling non-selling matters** (e.g. dealing with any complaints). These sales staff, therefore, need to be **fully trained** for personal selling to be effective.

Public relations (PR)

Strictly speaking, this is not part of promotion but is sometimes linked with it. This is because PR attempts to improve relations between a firm and people who may, or may not, be its customers. The PR department, therefore, uses **press releases** to publicise good points to do with the company, as well as becoming involved with '**image advertising**', where the company's name and image is promoted as well as (or even instead of) its products.

PROGRESS CHECK

1. Give **three** reasons why firms promote their products.
2. State **one** argument for, and **one** argument against, advertising.
3. Name **three** other forms of promotion.

3. Sales promotion; direct marketing; personal selling.
2. For: brings products to consumers' attention. Against: it can exploit consumers.
1. Introduce new products; increase sales of existing products; boost company image.

7.6 Place

LEARNING SUMMARY

After studying this section you should be able to understand:
- *the main types of channels of distribution*
- *services that wholesalers offer*
- *the types of retail outlets*
- *the nature of e-commerce*

Channels of distribution

Firms making products for particular markets have to decide how their products are to reach these markets. In doing so, they will make decisions about the method of **transport** to use, and about the **distribution channels** through which the product will pass.

The types of channel

The channels shown in Fig. 7.13 represent the main ways that manufactured goods pass from producer to consumer. Each channel includes the same activities: as well as the act of buying and selling, the product will be **promoted** at the various stages of distribution, **stored** for a time, and then **transported** to the next stage.

A producer may **sell directly** to the final consumer, as shown by channel A, and therefore omit both wholesaler and retailer. Some manufacturers run **factory shops** from which their products can be bought. Other forms of the 'manufacturer direct to final consumer' channel include the door-to-door selling

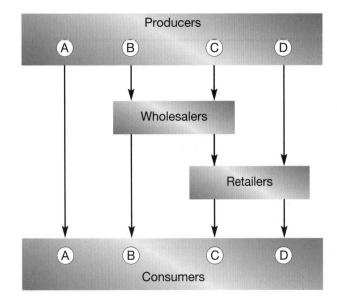

Fig. 7.12 The main channels of distribution

of some products (Avon cosmetics is a well-known example), **mail order selling** through agents who carry out some of the retailer's duties, farmers selling their products through 'pick-your-own' offers, and computer firms advertising their products in newspapers for sale directly to consumers.

In channel B, the retailer is avoided, the wholesaler receiving goods from the producer and then selling them to the final consumer. These wholesalers are usually based in densely populated areas, often selling consumer durables at low prices.

Channel C shows the traditional pattern. The manufacturer sells in bulk to wholesalers, who then resell in smaller quantities to retailers: these retailers sell single items to consumers. Many foodstuffs and finished goods are still sold through this traditional channel.

The wholesaler may be avoided by a producer, who then sells directly to large retailers (channel D). Retailers such as Tesco and B&Q, through their size, organise their own distribution and also carry out some of the functions of a wholesaler, e.g. by being able to store large quantities of goods. One popular development related to this channel is where producers set up their own retail outlets using **vertical forwards integration** (page 60). The **franchising** of retail outlets (page 40) is another important variation of this channel.

> Retailers need to be persuaded to stock products: they must consider the risk of selling (or not selling) the product, and the space it occupies.

Selecting the channel

The choice of channel largely depends on the product that is being distributed.

- **Consumer goods** use the above channels.
- **Raw materials** are often distributed through commodity exchanges, e.g. the London Metal Exchange which grades and sells a range of metals.
- Some **foodstuffs** are also sold either through a commodity exchange, through wholesale markets for fresh produce or by using specialist marketing and distribution boards, such as Milk Marque.
- A number of different channels are also used to sell **industrial goods**. There may be direct selling to the final consumer (e.g. the sales force using personal selling); or wholesalers or manufacturers' agents may be used to distribute items such as farm machinery and steel (e.g. steel stockholders).

> **KEY POINT**
>
> When deciding on the channel to use, the manufacturer considers two main points: the channel's cost, and the amount of control needed over distribution.

Wholesaling

AQA A   AQA B
EDEXCEL
OCR A   OCR B
WJEC
NICCEA

Services offered to manufacturers

1. **Bulk buying**. It is easier and cheaper for a manufacturer to deal with a few large orders, rather than with many small orders.

2. **Storage**. The producer's own warehousing costs are reduced.
3. **Promotion**. The wholesaler may promote the product on behalf of the manufacturer.
4. **Advice**. Feedback on the success of the goods can be given by the wholesaler.
5. **Risk-bearing**. The wholesaler, by acting as the manufacturer's market, takes on the risk of not being able to sell the goods.

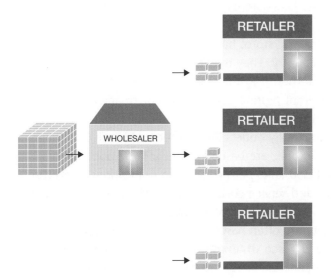

Fig. 7.13 Breaking bulk

Services offered to retailers

1. **Breaking bulk**. The wholesaler 'buys large' and 'sells small', saving the retailer the cost of holding large stocks.
2. **Selection**. The wholesaler typically has a range of manufacturer's goods from which the retailer can choose.
3. **Credit**. By granting credit, the wholesaler helps the retailer to finance the purchase. Some wholesalers operate as '**Cash and Carry**' outlets, where retailers get lower prices if they pay in cash for, and then collect and transport, their purchases.
4. **Information**. Product information is provided by the wholesaler.
5. **Delivery**. Many wholesalers are prepared to deliver to the retailer.

Survival of the wholesaler

Some channels of distribution now miss out the wholesaler. The large-scale retailers nowadays take on functions such as warehousing and breaking bulk, and so reduce the need for wholesalers. The fall in the number of smaller retailers has also reduced the demand for the traditional wholesaler.

Wholesalers have had to adapt to these changes. To help small shops be more competitive, **voluntary chains** such as Spar have been set up: wholesalers run the chain, supplying a large number of independent retailers with their goods. These retailers also benefit from national advertising, cheaper prices through bulk-buying, and 'own brand' goods.

> In particular, the cash-and-carry service offered by wholesalers has helped both themselves, and smaller retailers, to survive.

Retailing

Retailers also provide services to manufacturers and to consumers.

- **Services to manufacturers** include giving information about product sales, and storing the manufacturer's products.
- **Services to consumers** may include giving advice about products, as well as providing a local outlet, choice of product, and credit and delivery services.

Types of retail outlet

- **Independent retailers**. Although their overall importance has declined through competition from large-scale retailers such as Sainsbury, we still see many small retail shops often run as sole trader organisations (page 34) and specialising in a product or service, such as a local butcher or hairdresser.
- **Department stores**. A department store often operates as a plc (page 38), either as a single store or as a company such as Debenhams, found in a number of towns and cities. These stores have various departments selling a wide range of products.
- **Multiple stores**. These 'chain' stores have a head office and at least 10 branches throughout the country. They may be **specialist multiples**, such as Burtons specialising in clothes; they may operate as **variety multiples**, e.g. BhS, selling many different product lines. Food supermarkets are a particular type of specialist multiple store.
- **Discount stores**. We can classify outlets like Comet or Kwik-Fit as discount stores. They buy centrally in bulk, are based in or near large population centres ('out of town' rather than expensive city centre locations), advertise nationally, control display and service costs very carefully, and as a result can afford to sell their goods at low or discounted prices.
- **Retail superstores**. These are often based at out-of-town sites, with shops such as Sainsbury and Tesco **diversifying** from their traditional food sales into areas such as personal banking, savings, and the supply of consumer durables.

"Over the last three years, Sainsbury's Bank has attracted deposits of £1.6 billion and lent or made commitments of £1.5 billion with 1.25 million customers ... we've made access to the Bank's products even easier ... Our new Internet site at www.sainsburysbank.co.uk, due to be launched in June 2000, will also offer customers another way to conduct their financial affairs."

Fig. 7.14 Diversification by Sainsbury's (Source: J Sainsbury plc Annual Report and Accounts 2000)

- **Other types**. We know that **franchising** (page 40) is an increasingly common form of retail outlet; **co-operative retail societies** (page 39) and **voluntary chains** (page 139) are found; and other outlets include **mail order**, and **vending machines**.

An important trend for a number of retailers has been to offer their 'own-brand' products. Why are own-brand products so popular? A recent survey by the market research company Mori discovered the main reasons to be:

1. **price** – they are cheaper than market leader brands
2. **value for money** – based on consumers trusting the supermarket to offer value for money
3. **quality** – many consumers felt the quality matched the manufacturers' brands
4. **make** – many consumers realised that own-brand products are often made by the major manufacturers

Fig. 7.15 shows us another trend, towards fewer and larger retail outlets, and Fig. 7.16 summarises the differences in turnover.

Size of outlet	Number of businesses		Number of outlets		Turnover (£ million)	
	1996	1990	1996	1990	1996	1990
Single outlet retailers	181 880	215 793	181 880	215 793	40 270	34 533
Small multiple retailers (2–9 outlets)	23 906	25 492	64 487	65 802	24 334	14 723
Large multiple retailers (10 and more outlets)	1 177	903	74 257	68 252	128 632	77 624

Fig. 7.15 Retail outlets (Source: ONS)

Turnover	% of businesses	% share of total value of turnover
Up to £100 000	36	1
£100 000 to £999 999	59	5
£1 million to £10 million	4	8
Over £10 million	1	86
	100	100

Fig. 7.16 Retail businesses by turnover (1998)

KEY POINT

Important trends in retailing are the increasing diversification of superstores, the move towards self-service, the increase in 'own-brand' labels, and the development of out-of-town shopping centres.

e-commerce

Fig. 7.17 e-commerce takes off

> In 2000 Homebase, the 'DIY' store, was developing an £8 million home and garden website, which will feature home shopping.

'One strategic objective is to increase our e-commerce activities ... In June Sainsbury's Supermarkets will launch a major website, *Taste for Life*, which will be a huge source of recipe ideas and product information for customers ... Sainsbury's new upgraded home delivery and Internet shopping service *Sainsbury's to You* ... We are taking the opportunities of e-commerce very seriously ... We are giving a lot of thought to the implications of the growth of Internet shopping on the kind of stores that we operate and what customers will be looking for.'

Fig. 7.18 Sainsbury's interest in e-commerce (Source: Sainsbury's Group Chief Executive's Review, 2000)

Sainsbury's isn't alone: in 1999 Tesco, the UK's leading supermarket group, speeded up introducing its Internet shopping business into 100 stores. This followed the success of its Internet shopping scheme in 30 of its supermarkets, where it accounted for about 7% of the turnover. In another development at about the same time, the 'electronic shopping mall' named 'Open' started business on digital television. **e-commerce** is becoming very important as a means for companies – both large and small – to sell their products.

> **UK online for business is a government-led national initiative for UK e-commerce.**

Advantages of selling via the Internet or through digital television services are:

- **24-hour selling**, which makes it convenient for consumers who can shop at any time
- **low cost**, both to set up and to operate (for example, tills do not need to be staffed, and overheads such as rent are much lower)
- it is national and international, and so the company can **trade in new markets**
- **communication** is quite easy and often direct, e.g. via email addresses

The problems of e-commerce include:

> **Recent scares include a security breach that led to Barclays Bank having to shut down its online banking service in 2000.**

- a **lack of trust** by consumers when buying, particularly over the Internet
- world-wide customers may not understand English (which is the dominant Internet language), or may **lack access to the technology**
- customers **may not be aware** of the e-commerce site, e.g. through a lack of knowledge of how to search the Internet

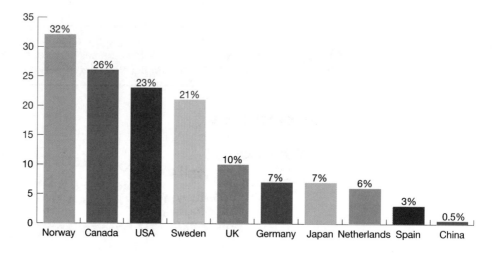

Fig. 7.19 Percentage of population using the Internet in 2000

Fig. 7.19 confirms that, world-wide, the rate of access to e-commerce outlets such as the Internet varies tremendously at present.

PROGRESS CHECK

1. List the services offered by a traditional wholesaler to:
   (a) a manufacturer
   (b) a retailer
2. State **three** major trends in modern retailing.

1. (a) Bulk buying; storage; promotion; advice; risk bearing
   (b) Breaking bulk; giving credit; selection; information; delivery
2. Decline in the number of small-scale retailers; growth in the sale of 'own-brand' labels; increased number of 'out-of-town', superstore shopping locations.

Sample GCSE questions

This is a question that tests you on three of the four Ps: pricing, promotion and place.

1. MyMouse Ltd. manufactures plastic casings and rubber mouse mats for computer 'mice'. The company now has the technology to start making personalised mouse mats: the computer user can send a photograph to the company's factory, the image on the photograph being copied onto the mouse mat. Although the personalised mouse mats will be expensive to make, they have proved very popular with the company's staff, and the directors do not know of any competitors in this area.

    The directors have a number of outlets they plan to use for the new personalised mouse mats:

    - their own small factory shop, where they sell mouse mats and casings to visitors
    - a small chain of computer shops, which currently sells their existing products
    - the Internet

(a) What pricing strategy would be appropriate for the new mouse mats? **(4)**

I think the pricing strategy should be penetration type. This is because MyMouse needs to capture a large market share if it is to sell its new mouse mats.

> This is a very limited answer. It would be better to refer to the unique nature of the product – there are no competitors – so 'skimming' or 'maximising' strategies may be stronger answers.

(b) Suggest how the directors might make customers aware of this new line. **(8)**

MyMouse needs to advertise. It can do this in a number of ways. I wouldn't recommend television because it's so expensive, although at Christmas people do advertise presents like personal mouse mats on the TV. There are other ways like cinema advertising but I think something local such as a local paper is best. This would be quite cheap and it is local, where MyMouse is.

> The reference to the local nature of the market is a good point here. The reference to Christmas is also appropriate, although this should be developed in the answer by relating it to suitable advertising media.

(c) Evaluate the suitability of each of the proposed outlets for the new mouse mats. **(12)**

Their own shop is a good idea, because people can bring along their photos and they can do it there and then. It is easy for the company because they don't have to send their mouse mats anywhere, they can get it done there. I would recommend the computer shops outlet because they already deal with them. Will they get as much profit, though? The computer shop owners will want some money for selling these mats, unlike the factory shop which belongs to MyMouse. The Internet is a great idea, because MyMouse computer mats are relevant to computers, which we need for the Internet. It means people all over the world can get these mats, though they will still have to send a photo or maybe send it electronically? The catch is the Internet is so massive now that not everyone will find out about MyMouse and its mats.

> Points should be made about (i) where these shops are located (transport costs / communication) and (ii) whether the shops can create the mats there or whether they have to communicate with MyMouse (time/expense). Mention that instructions can be given and orders made via the Internet, MyMouse can display its other products, it allows 24-hour sales and direct contact via email, and it can be a relatively cheap medium to use.

Exam practice questions

1. Which **three** of the following are the responsibilities of a company's marketing department? **(3)**

   N.B. *Do not tick more than **three** boxes.*

   Selecting new job applicants ☐   Carrying out market research ☐

   Quality control ☐   Looking after staff welfare ☐

   Ordering new equipment ☐   Paying suppliers ☐

   Promoting sales ☐   Planning production ☐

   Storing finished products ☐   Employing advertising agencies ☐

   WJEC Specimen Paper 1

2. Which **two** of the following are methods of desk research? **(2)**

   N.B. *Do not tick more than **two** boxes.*

   Reading trade journals ☐   Using consumer trials ☐

   Carrying out surveys ☐   Looking at Government statistics ☐

   Using telephone polls ☐   Carrying out opinion polls ☐

   WJEC Paper 1, 2000

3. SupaSlice Ltd is a company producing a wide range of bread products for the <u>mass market</u>, and cakes for special occasions such as weddings and 18th birthday parties. It sells most of its mass-market products through its own chain of shops in the Midlands, and the rest direct to catering establishments in this area. The company adds a percentage to its cost of manufacture to determine the price of these items, though some are sold as <u>loss leaders</u>. It uses a skimming pricing policy for its speciality products, which are promoted – with the company's bread products – through both <u>point-of-sale advertising</u> and advertisements in local papers.

   (a) Describe SupaSlice's marketing mix. **(4)**
   (b) Explain the **three** terms underlined in the data. **(6)**
   (c) Explain the difference in the company's approach to pricing its two types of product. **(6)**
   (d) Suggest **two** appropriate forms of market research for SupaSlice to use. **(4)**
   (e) The directors want to increase sales income. The Sales Director is considering increasing the selling price of cakes, but the Accountant suggests the company may be better off lowering the price.

   Explain **two** possible effects on SupaSlice Ltd arising from

   (i) increasing the selling price of cakes
   (ii) lowering the selling price of cakes **(4)**

Chapter 8 Production

The following topics are included in this chapter:

- **Methods of production**
- **Economies of scale**
- **Productivity**
- **Stock and quality control**

8.1 Methods of production

LEARNING SUMMARY

After studying this section you should be able to understand:

- **how production is organised**
- **lean production**
- **how production becomes 'lean'**

How production is organised

AQA A AQA B
EDEXCEL
OCR A OCR B
WJEC
NICCEA

The type of production a firm uses largely depends on the **scale** (size) of production with which it is involved.

Job production

> Examples of job production include building a ship, the Millennium Dome and a bridge such as the new Severn Bridge.

This is also called '**unit**' production. It is found when a business makes a **single unique product** from start to finish. The 'job' is based on the **individual specification** (the requirements and design) of the customer. Because of this:

Fig. 8.1 Job production: the Dome

- skilled labour is often used, and labour costs tend to be high because the work is **labour-intensive**
- employees have to be versatile, and flexible tools and equipment are often used
- economies of scale (see later) are not possible, so the finished product is often expensive

Firms using job production often find it difficult to calculate accurately the 'three Cs': the total **cost** of the job, the **cashflows** from it, and the job's **completion date**.

Batch production

> Examples of batch production include building similar houses on an estate, and making different styles of clothing or furniture.

Here, similar products are made in 'blocks', or **batches**. Production staff must make two key decisions: **how many** to make in each batch (**economic runs** are required to control costs), and **in what order** the various batches should be made.

Mass production

Other names for this are **flow-line** or **process** production. The products made using this method pass straight from one stage of production to the next. **Large numbers** of **identical, standardised products** are made as cheaply as possible, and economies of scale help the firm keep costs down. Where mass production takes place, the firm will:

- be **capital-intensive**, using **specialist machinery** and equipment
- employ staff who specialise in using this equipment
- keep production lines going **continuously** if possible (e.g. by shift work)
- be making high-demand products for a **mass market**
- rely on its **marketing function** to help sell the mass production

> The high capital (equipment) costs are affordable because the firm benefits from economies of scale.

> Examples of mass production include cars and many consumer durables, milk (and the cartons that the milk is put in), paint and petrol.

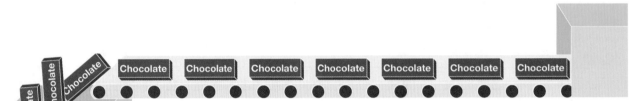

The layout of the production areas is important when mass production is used, because there is the need to minimise movement of parts and people. The production and assembly lines are therefore highly **automated**.

To sell products to a mass market, costs must be kept as low as possible. In addition to economies of scale, a mass manufacturer often uses **standard costing** (page 103) and **budgetary control** (page 106) to control costs.

Fig. 8.2 Mass production of chocolate bars

 KEY POINT Mass production relies on goods and services being traded as a result of specialisation and the division of labour.

Lean production

AQA A AQA B
EDEXCEL
OCR A OCR B
WJEC
NICCEA

We have known for many years that mass production causes several problems for firms. These include:

- staff becoming bored, and suffering from low morale
- labour and machinery being over-specialised, so the firm finds it difficult to respond to changes in its market
- equipment failure or employee action (e.g. strike action) being very costly, because it can halt all production

These drawbacks have led to a flexible '**lean production**' approach being used by many firms. A lean production approach sets out to:

- **reduce costs**, such as costs of holding stock and wasting stock
- **improve staff morale**, and therefore employee **productivity levels**
- **use capacity efficiently** (see page 151)
- **improve quality** (see page 154)

> Employees are also less skilled than their job production counterparts, which can cause problems for them if they lose their jobs.

 KEY POINT By achieving this, the firm will be in a better position to respond to changes in its market. Governments also want to ensure that their industries can compete internationally, so will encourage efficient techniques such as lean production.

How production becomes 'lean'

A firm's approach to lean production may be based on **cell production**, the **Kaizen** philosophy, and/or the **JIT** ('Just-In-Time') approach.

Cell production

The 'cell production' approach has developed from mass manufacture. It tries to overcome the problems of low morale that can affect employees who work on mass production lines.

Cell production divides a mass (continuous) production line into different 'cells'. Each cell is a self-contained unit that produces an identifiable part of the finished product.

> **KEY POINT** Staff in each cell feel that they are much more involved in the firm's overall production.

The Kaizen philosophy is, therefore, not limited to production and production staff, but should exist throughout a firm.

Kaizen

This is a Japanese term, and its ideas have become popular with many UK businesses. It is based on the belief that it is often **better to invest in the views and ideas of staff rather than in new resources** such as new equipment. Using the Kaizen approach, staff not only carry out their work: they all also **look for ways to improve their work**.

Groups must be set up to put the Kaizen approach into practice. For example, a shop-floor production cell may operate as a Kaizen team. These groups discuss production and other issues, and offer solutions.

> **KEY POINT** Staff in each cell feel that they are much more involved in the firm's overall production.

Japanese multinational car manufacturers in the UK, such as Nissan and Toyota, are good examples of companies using JIT.

Just-in-time (JIT)

This approach has also been influenced by Japanese work practices. It tries to **reduce stockholding costs**. This can be achieved if the firm can operate with **no buffer** ('reserve') **stock**.

The **kanban** order card system is an example of how the JIT approach can also influence a firm's own production. Let's assume the firm makes its own packaging for its products. When this packaging is made, it will be moved to the packing section: here, it may be kept in two separate containers. When one container is empty, it – with its kanban card – will be taken to where the packaging is made. The packaging now starts being made to go in this container, 'just-in-time' for when it is needed for the finished products (as the second container becomes empty).

In 2000, the 'fuel protest' led to deliveries being affected: this is a good example of the dangers of the JIT approach.

Advantages of JIT	Disadvantages of JIT
• holding and storage costs fall	• costs of ordering increase
• there will be less stock wastage	• the firm relies totally on its suppliers
• cash flow (liquidity) improves production	• a delivery problem will stop

> **PROGRESS CHECK**
>
> 1. Which of the following products would normally be produced using mass production techniques: bridges; made-to-measure double-glazed windows; paving slabs; TVs; cars?
> 2. What does efficient 'Just-In-Time' production depend on?
>
> 1. TVs and cars. Bridges and windows illustrate job production, and slabs are likely to be made in batches.
> 2. For JIT to work efficiently, a firm must have very close working relationships with its suppliers, since frequent deliveries of satisfactory-quality stocks are needed.

8.2 *Economies of scale*

> **LEARNING SUMMARY**
>
> After studying this section you should be able to understand:
> - *internal economies of scale*
> - *external economies of scale*
> - *diseconomies of scale*

Internal economies of scale

Producing on a large scale brings many benefits to a firm. These 'economies of scale' result from a **falling average cost per unit** made.

Internal economies of scale

These economies occur as a result of something that is internal to – **inside** – the firm, which reduces its average costs.

How can average costs fall? As a firm's output and its scale of operation increases, this increased output does not normally increase the firm's **fixed costs** (see page 102). This means that these fixed costs are spread over a larger output, and so the average cost per unit falls. Here's an illustration: if a firm's rent (fixed cost) is £100 000 a year and it makes 50 000 items in 2001, its average fixed cost per item is £2. If it then makes 100 000 in 2002, this average fixed cost falls to £1 for each item made.

Here are some examples of internal economies of scale leading to lower unit costs.

- **Economies of increased dimensions** – these arise from an increase in size: for example, oil companies use 'supertankers' that can have 20 times the capacity of smaller ships, yet cost only three or four times as much to build and to run.
- **Financial economies** – larger firms are assumed to be more stable financially, and therefore find it easier to obtain loan capital. They can negotiate lower interest rates on these loans. Larger companies (plcs) also have more, often less expensive, sources of finance available.
- **Managerial economies** – Highly qualified, **expert managers** can be employed by larger-scale firms. Also, the cost of management will not increase at the same rate as the growth of the firm: if it doubles in size, it will still only have one managing director, one sales director and so on.

> This is another example of the division of labour.

twice the size…
…but not twice the running costs

Fig. 8.3 Economy of increased dimensions

- **Marketing economies** – larger firms can afford to buy the services of **specialist marketing** companies such as advertising agencies. The costs of promotion are spread over more sales, which can reduce their unit cost.
- **Purchasing economies** – larger firms receive **bulk-buying** discounts, which lower unit costs. They can also negotiate more favourable (cheaper) credit terms with suppliers.
- **Risk-bearing economies** – firms grow larger through increasing their product range: this **diversification** spreads the risk across more markets and more products.
- **Technical economies** – firms with large-scale production can use **more advanced machinery** (or use existing machinery more efficiently). A larger firm can also more easily afford to invest in **research and development**, which may improve its products.

External economies of scale

> A good example is the Midlands, where we find many suppliers of components to the local car industry.

> Examples include 'Sheffield steel', china from the Potteries and financial services (London).

When the whole **industry** grows in size, its firms can gain from this growth in these ways.

- **Information**. Firms in the area often link together to provide joint information (and also research and development) schemes, supported by their local trade associations and chambers of commerce.
- **Concentration**. Where the industry is based mainly in one area, this can encourage suppliers to locate in the same area.
- **Skilled staff**. Through 'concentration', labour and management gain specialist local skills: these are developed further by specialist local training schemes.
- **Reputation**. A local or regional good reputation can help firms in that region, and encourage other firms to locate there.

Diseconomies of scale

AQA A **AQA B**
EDEXCEL
OCR A **OCR B**
WJEC
NICCEA

Although there are many benefits that come from increased size, there are limits to these benefits. Firms may grow too large, and start to suffer from **diseconomies** as their **unit costs increase**. These diseconomies arise for a number of reasons.

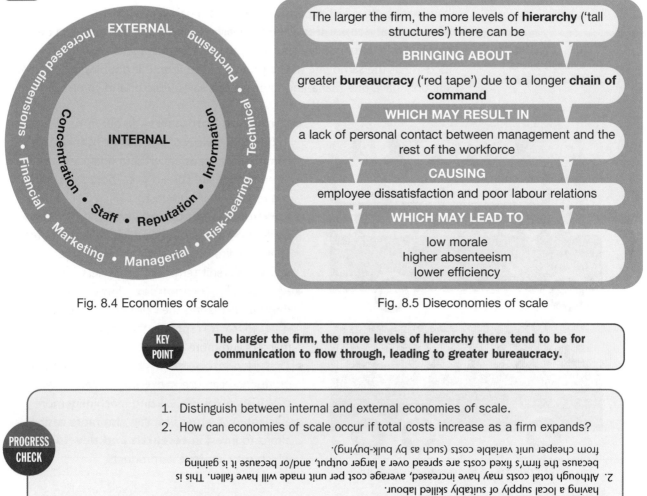

Fig. 8.4 Economies of scale   Fig. 8.5 Diseconomies of scale

KEY POINT The larger the firm, the more levels of hierarchy there tend to be for communication to flow through, leading to greater bureaucracy.

PROGRESS CHECK

1. Distinguish between internal and external economies of scale.
2. How can economies of scale occur if total costs increase as a firm expands?

2. Although total costs may have increased, average cost per unit made will have fallen. This is because the firm's fixed costs are spread over a larger output, and/or because it is gaining from cheaper unit variable costs (such as by bulk-buying).

1. Internal are within the firm itself. External occur when all the firms in the area benefit, such as having a local supply of suitably skilled labour.

8.3 Productivity

LEARNING SUMMARY

After studying this section you should be able to understand:

● *using productive capacity efficiently*
● *using technology efficiently*

Using productive capacity efficiently

AQA A **AQA B**
EDEXCEL
OCR A **OCR B**
WJEC
NICCEA

A firm's **productivity** tells us how efficient it is at producing its products. We can measure the productivity of the workforce, e.g. by measuring the average number of products made per employee.

We also need to measure how productive the firm's non-human resources are.

Productive capacity

A firm's 'productive capacity' refers to its resources: in particular, its **premises**, the **machinery and equipment** it has, and its **workforce**. If all are working at their maximum output, the firm is said to be operating at its **full capacity**.

As with economies of scale, the firm gains if it can **spread its fixed costs over greater output**. If it can do this, its unit costs will fall. The more efficient the firm's use of its capacity, the lower its unit costs will be.

Working at or near full capacity can, however, create problems for a firm. There is:

- pressure on **staff** – this can lead to greater absenteeism, e.g. through stress caused by high workloads
- pressure on **equipment** – e.g. extra use causes more wear and tear, leading to equipment breakdown with production being affected
- pressure when **additional work** is taken on – if a firm is working at or near full capacity, it is difficult to find additional capacity

> **Firms in this position often employ more part-time staff (e.g. seasonal workers) or hire/buy extra premises and equipment.**

Other firms may have to **reduce excess capacity**. This becomes necessary when demand for their products falls permanently. Ways of reducing excess staff include 'natural wastage' (not replacing leavers), and non-human resources can be reduced, e.g. by moving to smaller and cheaper premises.

> **KEY POINT**
>
> Production tries to turn input into output as efficiently as possible: this is a measure of the firm's productivity.

Using technology efficiently

AQA A AQA B
EDEXCEL
OCR A OCR B
WJEC
NICCEA

It is important for a firm's **technology** to be as productive as possible. Many firms use new technologies in the production process. Examples include:

- **computer-aided design** (CAD) packages are used to create efficient product designs that can be altered immediately, by using light pens or touch-sensitive screens
- **computer-aided manufacture** (CAM) uses robotics and other forms of automation to make products efficiently

> **KEY POINT**
>
> The more technology-based (capital-intensive) a firm becomes, the fewer staff it will employ: there can be a 'trade-off' between equipment (capital) and jobs (labour). The nature of the jobs – skills involved, training required etc. – also change as a firm's use of technology changes.

> **PROGRESS CHECK**
>
> 1. What is the difference between 'production' and 'productivity'?
> 2. What are the elements involved in measuring productive capacity?
>
> 2. Productive capacity is a measure of the firm's use of its human resources and its non-human resources (buildings, equipment etc.).
> 1. 'Production' refers to how many (and what types) are made; 'productivity' relates to how efficient the firm is at making what it does make.

8.4 Stock and quality control

After studying this section you should be able to understand:

- *buying*
- *stock control*
- *quality*

Buying

AQA A   AQA B
EDEXCEL
OCR A   OCR B
WJEC
NICCEA

Both manufacturing and non-manufacturing firms have to make all sorts of purchases. The range of responsibility of a typical purchasing department is shown in Fig. 8.7.

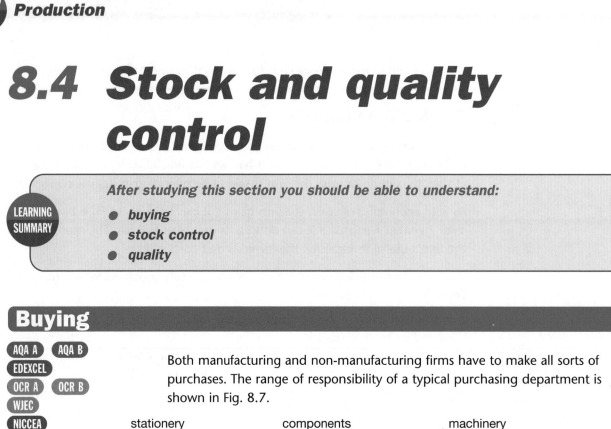

Fig. 8.6 Role of the purchasing department

The main role of the purchasing department is, therefore, **materials management**. The items bought must be 'correct' in many ways – they must be:

- bought in the **correct quantities**
- bought at the **correct price**
- bought at the **correct level of quality**
- delivered to the **correct place**
- delivered at the **correct time**

Stock control

AQA A   AQA B
EDEXCEL
OCR A   OCR B
WJEC
NICCEA

Firms have to **hold** sufficient stocks for a number of reasons.

Stock item	Reason	Costs of zero stock
raw materials and work in progress	to meet production requirements	idle time (worker and machine); knock-on effect of delayed production
finished goods	to meet customer demand	loss of goodwill and orders; financial penalties for missing deadlines
consumables, spares, equipment	to support sales and production	idle time (worker and machine); delayed production

Firms also need to manage their stock efficiently. The oldest stock will normally be used first (stock rotation), and stock wastage must be minimised.

There are conflicting 'pulls' in the firm, which influence buying and stock control policies. Purchasing departments have to balance the need to keep costs under control, but also ensure that stock is always available.

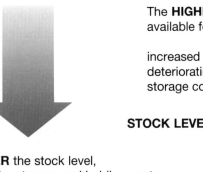

The **HIGHER** the stock level, the more stock available for production
BUT
increased risks of stock becoming out-of-date, deteriorating or being stolen; and increased storage costs

STOCK LEVELS

The **LOWER** the stock level, the lower the storage and holding costs
BUT
increasing risk of running out of stock and production stopping

Fig. 8.7 The 'pulls' in stock control

Optimum stock

The 'best' stock level – the optimum stock – is the level that **minimises costs**. There are four control levels used to calculate optimum stock.

1. **Reorder quantity**. The **EOQ** (Economic Order Quantity) is the number of items of stock the firm will reorder, once the reorder stock level has been reached. The EOQ is calculated by comparing the costs the firm would face by holding a lot of stock, with the savings it gets from buying this stock in bulk.
2. **Reorder level**. This is the level at which a new order will be made.
3. **Minimum stock**. This is the **buffer** stock level, below which the stock level should not fall.
4. **Maximum stock**. This is the highest level of stock that the firm will hold.

Stock control charts can be constructed to show these levels.

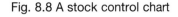

Fig. 8.8 A stock control chart

KEY POINT

The EOQ calculation is based on a number of 'constant' assumptions: a constant demand for the stock; a constant lead time (the time between placing an order and receiving it); and costs of making an order are constant, regardless of order size.

Quality

AQA A   AQA B

EDEXCEL

OCR A   OCR B

WJEC

NICCEA

> Quality circles (closely linked to the Kaizen philosophy) are an example of quality assurance: they are employee groups with a common interest, who meet to discuss quality-related work issues.

> Quality control forms an important part of production control.

Quality assurance and quality control

Satisfying customers is necessary for success: quality assurance tries to achieve this by **agreeing** and **implementing quality standards** throughout a firm.

The purpose of quality control is to ensure that **standards are** (at least) **being maintained**. It is particularly associated with traditional flow-line production. A recent trend has been for employees to adopt a **self-checking** approach: this is an example of the **people-centred management** philosophy, that quality is the responsibility of all employees.

Quality control tries to:

- **stop** problems from arising in the first place
- **detect** quality problems before the goods reach the customer
- **correct** problems and procedures
- **improve** quality to meet higher customer expectations

Quality initiatives

Benchmarking measures a firm's production or other activity against the **industry standard**. It looks for 'best practice' from other firms, and managers can compare this practice to that of their firm. By using benchmarking:

- managers can set **realistic targets**
- staff can become **motivated** through greater involvement
- management becomes aware if the firm is at a **competitive disadvantage**

Total Quality Management (TQM) seeks to establish a 'quality culture' that assures the quality of work of all staff at all stages of production and sale. It is a philosophy associated with quality circles, and which emphasises the importance of after-sales service.

The **International Standards Organisation** sets requirements for a quality framework within a firm. This includes making firms document procedures in a quality manual, and requiring them to evaluate their quality systems.

> **KEY POINT**
>
> The more efficient firms believe that it is better to 'get it right first time', to avoid the costs, delays and loss of orders that come from getting it wrong.

 PROGRESS CHECK

1. Name **four** items that a typical manufacturing firm has to buy.
2. A purchasing department must provide the correct items in the correct _____ , at the correct _____ and the correct _____ , and also ensure they are delivered to the correct _____ at the correct _____ .

2. Quantity, price, quality, place, time.
1. Raw materials; office stationery; manufacturing machinery; company cars.

Sample GCSE questions

This question is about methods of production, and stock and quality control.

The *Ice Cream Farm* makes and sells a range of ice cream and frozen yoghurt products. It is still based next to the original owner's farm, from where it gets some of its ingredients. The firm has sold its products locally for many years, but nowadays uses specialised production lines for these products. The packing process uses the mass (continuous flow) method, but produces identifiable batches of flavoured yoghurt and ice cream. The firm attaches great importance to its quality control, and has recently introduced computers to help control the production process, and stock levels in both the factory shop and the warehouse.

1. **Using examples**, explain the terms:

    (a) batch production (3)

    Batch production is found where a number of the same things are made at a time.
    Examples include wallpaper, lamp shades, garden furniture, different types of loaves and cakes.

    > *This just about explains what batch production is. The answer should point out that, once one batch is completed, another batch of a different product/line will be made. These are good examples.*

    (b) mass (continuous flow) production (3)

    Mass, or continuous flow, production involves making things all the time. It is widely found in the UK. Examples include making chemicals, liquids such as petrol from oil refining, and the sort of things you buy in `do-it-yourself` stores.

    > *Make sure you give a clearer definition than 'making things all the time': mention the mass production aspect, and how the products made pass straight from one process to the next ('continuous' is the key). Good examples mentioned to start with, but the reference to DIY stores is too vague, so give examples from these stores such as light bulbs, nails, paints.*

2. Why should the *Ice Cream Farm* be so concerned about quality control? (4)

    Where a company is making things such as ice cream or other food and drinks, it has to be very careful to ensure that they are safe to eat and drink. If the company finds that it is making ice cream that isn't safe to eat, it will lose a lot of custom and may go out of business.

    > *This is a good start, though more could be made of the results of selling poor quality products – customers look elsewhere, market share is lost, profits fall and the survival of the firm is in question.*

3. Why does the *Ice Cream Farm* have to control its stocks? (6)

    The Ice Cream Farm must monitor its stocks because it needs to make sure that it does not have too much stock, nor too little. The effect of the Farm having too much stock is that money is wasted in holding too much, space is tied up, and the stocks may go off or be stolen. If the company has too little stock, it may not have enough to keep making using a continuous flow process.

    > *You also need to explain the effect of not being able to meet production targets: loss of deliveries = loss of sales orders and loss of future orders.*

Exam practice questions

This is a question on methods of production and economies of scale.

1. Bildit is a manufacturer of modern household furniture, and the company is moving to a new factory. The managing director has to decide the method of production to make the products in the new factory.

(a) (i) State how the furniture would be made if the managing director decided on job production. (2)

....

....

   (ii) Explain **one** advantage and **one** disadvantage of job production for Bildit. (4)

....

....

....

....

(b) Explain why, if flow production is used, Bildit could benefit from economies of scale. (6)

....

....

....

....

....

....

(c) Which method should the managing director decide on? Give reasons for your answer. (4)

....

....

....

....

Exam practice answers

Chapter 1

1.

(a) There is an ageing population: seen in an increase in the 46 and over age groups (from 40% to 54%) and a fall in the 45 and under segment (from 60% to 46%). Since the younger age groups will soon comprise less than half the local population, compared with three in five at present, this will affect demand for the Centre's services (likely to be higher in the younger age range). There will also be a switch from sporting activities demanded by younger people (eg gymnasia) to the more leisure-based ones demanded by older people, or to sport they can undertake more gently (e.g. swimming). There may also be a change in demand for, and income from, membership.

(b) The Centre should review its facilities to ensure it can adapt to these changing demands. It should also review how and where it advertises its services, and the type of membership it offers, to encourage more older people to join and attend.

Chapter 2

1.

The name of the company is followed by the letters 'plc' X	The name of the company is followed by the letters 'Ltd'
The maximum number of shareholders is 20	Shares are sold on the Stock Exchange X
Shares cannot be sold to members of the general public	They have a minimum share capital of £50 000 X
They are owned by the government on behalf of the public	They have unlimited liability

2. **(d)** have unlimited liability **(f)** share responsibilities between the owners   **(g)** do not have more than 20 owners
   (i) share the workload between the owners

Chapter 3

1.

(a) Buying (Purchasing)

(b) **(i)** The number of staff controlled by one person
   (ii) 8 office staff   **(iii)** The Managing Director
   (iv) The Finance Director

(c) It confirms the status of the individual staff, and shows the formal lines of communication.

(d) **(i)** Sales: responsible for marketing and promoting the firm's existing products, and for market research into proposed new products.
   (ii) Accounts: responsible for the control of finance and the production of financial information; may also be responsible for credit control.

Chapter 4

1.

(a) Increased output levels through increased efficiency, which can lead to higher sales.

(b) British Trade International can support Merchant Electronics by providing information and advice. The Export Credit Guarantee Department can support the company by providing guarantees and insurance against loss.

(c) New working conditions, about which the unions will want to negotiate. Also, they will want negotiations concerning any redeployment or redundancy of existing staff, and to ensure staff receive adequate training. Pay may also need renegotiating. There may be health and safety issues to be discussed.

Chapter 5

1.

(a) Pay negotiations: unions negotiate with management, locally or nationally. Working conditions: unions seek to improve working conditions/environment.

(b) Normal pay rate £7 x 40 hours   = £280
   Overtime rate £10.50 x 10 hours   = £105
   Total pay   = £385

(c) Machines are likely to take the place of labour; machines are likely to operate more quickly and efficiently.

(d) If machines are more efficient, Gripabag's goods can be sold at lower prices, making them more competitive. The company is more likely to make a profit and possibly expand, therefore needing more staff (or allowing existing staff to keep their jobs). What Gripabag has to do is to get enough income and profit to finance the new machines, otherwise the company may face problems of survival.

2.

(a) **(i)** A record of an individual's education, employment experience and other interests.
   (ii) Because the job requires up-to-date computer skills, so the company wants evidence of an applicant's ability to work with computers.

(b) **(i)** Aptitude test: to check a candidate's suitability for the work, e.g. by providing a series of computer-based tests. Intelligence tests: to see if the candidate's IQ is near that expected for this position.
   (ii) The aptitude test will allow Garfield Print to compare the results of the candidates' work on computers, giving them valuable evidence they can use.

(c) It allows candidates to explain any points the interviewers wish to ask. It allows both parties to make sure the job is suitable for the candidate and the candidate is suitable for the job.

(d) **(i)** It states the conditions under which the person is employed.
   (ii) Job title; names of both parties; rate of pay; holidays.

(e) **(i)** Decision-making is quicker. Communication is more efficient.
   (ii) Tall hierarchical structure.

Chapter 6

1. (a) The output at which total costs and total revenue are the same.

(b)

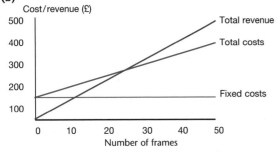

Fixed costs per fair £150 (wages, rent, travel); selling price £10 so total revenue £500 at 50 frames; variable costs £250 at 50 frames so £400 total costs (150 + 250).

(c) Break-even point shown on the graph is 30 frames.
Proof: contribution is £5 (£10 selling price - £5 cost);
break-even = £150 divided by £5 = 30 frames.

(d) The graph shows £100 profit, difference between total revenue and total costs. Proof: total revenue = 50 x £10 = £500; fixed costs £150 and variable costs £250 (50 x £5), so total costs = £400 and profit = £100.

(e) Jeff's total income per fair is £200 (£100 wages + £100 profit): he needs to attend 75 fairs (£15 000 divided by £200).

(f) The major problems are likely to include: at present, insufficient equipment owned to make the number required for the new order; a limited amount of capital to invest in the new equipment needed; a lack of storage and other space; and a lack of time and staff to make the required number. Jeff could consider:

- obtaining larger premises (but cost of buying/renting ...)
- obtaining additional equipment (but cost of buying/renting again ...)
- arranging loans (but lender may want detailed financial statements; may not give loan ...)
- taking on a partner (need to find one; may not work well together; still have unlimited liability ...)
- employing staff (may need training in wages/payroll procedures ...)
- looking to family/friends for capital (but may cause domestic and friendship problems ...)

Chapter 7

1. Promoting sales, carrying out market research, employing advertising agencies.

2. Reading trade journals, looking at Government statistics.

3.

(a) 'Marketing mix' refers to the 'four Ps': product, price, place and promotion. In this example, the products are the range of food items made: perishable, either high-turnover (bread) or one-off/batch (cakes) items marketed mainly to the general public. Prices are based on cost-plus (bread) and skimming (cakes), and it uses loss leaders as part of its pricing policy in order to attract sales. 'Place' refers to the market outlets: its own shops, and catering establishments in the Midlands. Promotion is by loss leaders, and advertising both in local newspapers and at the point of sale.

(b) 'Mass market' refers to a highly populated, general market, such as the one associated with mainstream food products such as bread. 'Loss leaders' occur where a firm sells one of its product lines at a price below cost, in order to attract custom in the hope that consumers will also buy other items. 'Point-of-sale advertising' occurs at the point of sale (e.g. at a shop counter in this example).

(c) Bread is sold at 'cost-plus', where a set percentage is added to the cost of the individual product to obtain the selling price. Although this ensures production costs are met and there is a contribution towards overheads, competitors' prices may be ignored, resulting in an uncompetitive price for the firm's products. Cakes are sold at a 'skimming' price, ie a high price that recognises the uniqueness of the product (or, in this case, there may be a local monopoly). This strategy may encourage competitors to enter the local market, forcing the firm to lower its prices in order to compete.

(d) The company could use either street surveys of in-store test marketing. The advantage of street surveys is that they could be conducted close to local SupaSlice shops, thus surveying actual and potential consumers. Test marketing would allow the company staff to talk directly to those already committed to buying its products: this would give immediate and direct feedback, and be relatively inexpensive.

(e) This depends on the elasticity of demand for the company's cake products. Increasing the price would increase total revenue if demand was inelastic (i.e. sales only fall a relatively small amount), but elastic demand would lead to a fall in total revenue. If the price is reduced, an elastic demand should increase total revenue (many more sales are made), but an inelastic demand will lead to a fall in revenue (the number of cakes sold increases only marginally). If either policy results in lower income, this could affect the company's cash flow and employment prospects for staff.

Chapter 8

1.

(a) (i) Staff employed in making the furniture complete the item, i.e. work from start to finish on it.

(ii) Advantage: staff tend to be more interested in the work; disadvantage, slow method of production.

(b) A larger output is made, allowing e.g. bulk buying of materials, efficient specialist equipment to be used. This means that the fixed costs are spread over a larger output, reducing the average cost of production.

(c) Flow production, assuming there is a sufficient market for the products. Job production if the company is selling on the basis of 'quality', though this may be unlikely ('modern household furniture' suggests a mass market).

Index

Index